Foods of America

AROUND AMERICA'S KITCHENS

D0488594

MARKS &
SPENCER

INTRODUCTION 7

BACK ON THE HOMESTEAD... 8
Farmhouse breakfast 10
Hearty soups 16
Beef dishes 18
Lamb dishes 22
Pork dishes 24
Poultry 26
Side dishes 30
Home-baked pies 34
A cool drink on the porch... 38

TEX-MEX
Ranch-style breakfast
Spicy soups
Salsas & dips
Snacks
It's all about tortillas...
Classic chilli
Sticky ribs
Rice & beans
Sundownwers... and risers

A TASTE OF THE DEEP SOUTH
Soups & stews
Corn bread
Finger lickin' ribs
Soul Food
Southern-style chicken
Straight off the grill
Shrimp boats are a comin'...
Crab & lobster
On the side
Deep South desserts
Southern coolers

DINER SPECIALS
All-day breakfast
Pancakes & hotcakes
Waffles
Sandwiches
Bagels & melts
Grill plate specials
Side order of potatoes
A slice of pie
Ice cream sundaes
Milkshakes & malts

GREAT AMERICAN CLASSICS
Brunch
Chowder
Salads & dressings
Seafood platter
Wings 'n' ribs
Burgers & hot dogs
Steaks
Thanksgiving
As American as...
All-American desserts
Classic cocktails

JUST LIKE MOM USED TO BAKE
Cookies
Muffins
Brownies & blondies
Cupcakes
Chocolate cakes
Sunday-best cakes
Cheesecakes
Fruity loaves
Candy & sweet treats

GLOSSARY
INDEX
CONVERSION CHARTS

Introduction

American food is perhaps the finest example of 'fusion' foods. The people arriving to live in America since the 1600s come from all over the world, and each group brings with them their own recipes, styles of cooking, ingredients and even the seeds or roots with which to grow the food. So now, North America grows potatoes, rice, avocados and so many more things which originated on very distant shores.

This all goes to make for a fascinating culinary journey around the United States – we have chosen to take you through just a few of the real hallmark dishes of America, by looking at where you might find them – a diner in San Francisco or New York is likely to serve broadly similar foods, with local variations; there are those dishes which are just 'classic American' and are likely to be found almost anywhere; and then of course Tex-Mex recipes originated in the state of Texas, but as populations moved and took their food with them, increasingly Tex-Mex dishes and the use of chillies, found their way to many other States as well.

Where a recipe calls for beans, we often assume the use of dried beans, which normally need overnight soaking. However, tinned beans can be substituted. Similarly, corn is used in some recipes – we talk about cooking the cob and stripping it, but you could equally use the same quantity of tinned or frozen corn kernels. Bagels and sourdough are amongst the staples of American bakeries – we include recipes for these, but you could also use shop-bought versions for ease and speed. And where we specify grill plate or barbecue, alternatively you can use a griddle plate on top of the cooker, grilling under a conventional grill, or for barbecuing, roast in the oven. We also give fat and calorie counts in all our recipes, except for desserts and drinks.

Find the ingredients you like, mix and match your textures, tastes, spices and dressings: the foods of America are not a precise cuisine. Make a recipe delightfully personal and make it your very own! Enjoy!

Back on the homestead...

When American settlers arrived in the west they brought with them recipes from many countries and adapted them for the New World. The ingredients had to be easy to get and the dishes had to appeal to the entire family. With fruit pies cooling on the windowsill, the smell of hot corncakes wafting across the yard and a bubbling pot of rich stew cooking on the stove, they soon made the wild country their home and their recipes became American classics.

Farmhouse breakfast

BUCKWHEAT PANCAKES WITH CARAMELISED BANANA

¼ cup (35g) self-raising flour
¼ cup (35g) buckwheat flour
1 tablespoon caster sugar
¼ teaspoon ground cinnamon
1 egg
¾ cup (180ml) skimmed milk
20g butter
¼ cup (50g) firmly packed brown sugar
4 medium bananas (800g), sliced thickly
2 tablespoons water

1 Combine flours, caster sugar and cinnamon in medium bowl; gradually whisk in combined egg and milk until smooth. Cover; refrigerate 30 minutes.
2 Meanwhile, melt butter in large frying pan. Add brown sugar; cook, stirring, until dissolved. Add banana and the water; cook, uncovered, stirring occasionally, about 2 minutes or until banana is caramelised.
3 Pour ¼ cup (60ml) of the batter into heated 20cm non-stick frying pan; cook pancake until browned both sides. Repeat with remaining batter to make four pancakes; cover to keep warm. Just before serving, halve each pancake and divide among serving plates. Spoon banana mixture onto each half; fold to enclose filling. Drizzle with remaining sauce.

preparation time 10 minutes
(plus refrigeration time)
cooking time 20 minutes
serves 4
per serving 6.1g fat; 1285kj (307 cal)

tips Fresh strawberries may be used as a filling instead of caramelised bananas. Dust pancakes with icing sugar before serving.

BUTTERMILK PANCAKES WITH MAPLE SYRUP CREAM

1 cup (150g) self-raising flour
½ teaspoon ground cinnamon
1 tablespoon caster sugar
2 eggs, beaten lightly
1¼ cups (310ml) buttermilk
125g reduced-fat smooth ricotta cheese
½ cup (125ml) maple syrup
1 medium lemon (140g), cut into wedges

1 Sift flour, cinnamon and sugar into medium bowl. Whisk in combined egg and buttermilk, gradually, until smooth. Cover; stand 30 minutes.
2 Pour ¼ cup (60ml) of the batter into heated oiled non-stick frying pan; cook until bubbles start to appear. Turn pancake; cook until browned underneath. Remove pancake from pan; cover to keep warm. Repeat with remaining batter to make eight pancakes.
3 Combine ricotta with a tablespoon of the maple syrup in small bowl.
4 Serve pancakes with ricotta mixture, remaining maple syrup and lemon.

preparation time 10 minutes
(plus standing time)
cooking time 10 minutes
serves 4
per serving 7.6g fat; 1599kj (382 cal)

BUTTERMILK PANCAKES

'He who goes to bed hungry dreams of pancakes.'
American proverb

Pancakes are the classic American breakfast. They are served with a variety of toppings – from fruit sauces to slices of crisp bacon, but undoubtedly the most popular is maple syrup.

Store eggs in refrigerator with ends pointing down so the yolk is less likely to break when egg is used. As eggshells are porous they should not be washed before storing or be stored near strong-smelling foods. Before using eggs in a recipe, break one at a time into a small saucer, that way, a stale egg can be discarded, rather than ruin the whole dish.

SCRAMBLED EGGS ON CORN CAKES

SCRAMBLED EGGS ON CORN CAKES

1 trimmed corn cob (250g)
¾ cup (110g) plain flour
1 teaspoon sweet paprika
1 tablespoon finely chopped fresh
coriander
¼ cup (60ml) milk
3 egg whites
3 eggs
2 egg whites, extra

1 Cut corn kernels from cob. Combine corn, flour, paprika and coriander in medium bowl; stir in milk.
2 Beat the 3 egg whites in small bowl with electric mixer until soft peaks form; fold into corn mixture. Cook ¼-cup measures of corn mixture in heated oiled large frying pan until browned both sides and cooked through.
3 Using fork, lightly beat whole eggs and extra egg whites in medium bowl. Cook egg mixture in medium lightly oiled frying pan, stirring gently, until just set.
4 Serve scrambled eggs with corn cakes.

preparation time 20 minutes
cooking time 15 minutes
serves 4
per serving 5.4g fat; 957kj (229 cal)

BAKED BEANS WITH FRIED EGGS

1 cup (200g) dried borlotti beans
3 bacon rashers (210g), rind removed,
chopped coarsely
1 medium onion (150g), chopped finely
1 clove garlic, crushed
1 tablespoon tomato paste
400g can crushed tomatoes
1½ cups (375ml) water
1 tablespoon worcestershire sauce
2 teaspoons american mustard
1 tablespoon pure maple syrup
4 eggs

1 Place beans in medium bowl, cover with cold water; soak overnight, drain.
2 Cook bacon, onion and garlic in large pan, stirring, until onion softens. Add drained beans with paste, undrained tomatoes, the water, sauce and mustard; bring to a boil. Reduce heat; simmer, covered, about 1½ hours. Uncover; simmer about 15 minutes or until beans soften. Stir in syrup.
3 Fry eggs in heated oiled medium frying pan until white has set and yolk is cooked as desired. Serve beans with eggs.

preparation time 10 minutes
(plus soaking time)
cooking time 2 hours 10 minutes
serves 4
per serving 12.9g fat; 1287kj (308 cal)
tips Dried beans are soaked overnight to help them cook faster, improve their flavour and texture, and make them easier to digest.

CHEESE, CORN & BACON MUFFINS

½ cup (85g) polenta
½ cup (125ml) milk
3 bacon rashers (210g), rind removed, chopped finely
4 spring onions, chopped finely
1½ cups (225g) self-raising flour
1 tablespoon caster sugar
310g can corn kernels, drained
125g can creamed corn
100g butter, melted
2 eggs, beaten lightly
50g piece cheddar cheese
¼ cup (30g) coarsely grated cheddar cheese

1 Preheat oven to 180°C/160°C fan-assisted. Oil 12-hole (⅓-cup/80ml) muffin pan.
2 Mix polenta and milk in small bowl, cover; stand 20 minutes.
3 Meanwhile, cook bacon, stirring, in heated small frying pan for 2 minutes. Add onion to pan; cook, stirring, for another 2 minutes. Remove pan from heat; cool 5 minutes.
4 Sift flour and sugar into large bowl; stir in corn kernels, creamed corn and bacon mixture. Add melted butter, eggs and polenta mixture; mix muffin batter only until just combined.
5 Spoon 1 tablespoon of the batter into each hole of muffin pan. Cut piece of cheese into 12 equal pieces; place one piece in the centre of each muffin pan hole. Divide remaining batter among pan holes; sprinkle grated cheese over each.
6 Bake muffins about 20 minutes. Turn onto wire rack. Serve muffins warm.

preparation time 20 minutes
(plus standing time)
cooking time 20 minutes
makes 12
per muffin 12.5g fat 1087kj (260 cal)

PUMPKIN SCONES

40g butter
¼ cup (55g) caster sugar
1 egg, beaten lightly
¾ cup cooked mashed pumpkin
2½ cups (375g) self-raising flour
½ teaspoon ground nutmeg
⅓ cup (180ml) milk, approximately

1 Preheat oven to 220°C/200°C fan-assisted. Grease two 20cm-round sandwich tins.
2 Beat butter and sugar in small bowl with electric mixer until light and fluffy; beat in egg.
3 Transfer mixture to large bowl. Stir in pumpkin, then sifted dry ingredients and enough milk to make a soft sticky dough. Knead dough on floured surface until smooth.
4 Use hand to press dough out evenly to 2cm thickness. Cut as many 5cm rounds as you can from dough. Place rounds side by side, just touching, in pans. Gently knead scraps of dough together; repeat pressing and cutting of dough, place in same pan. Brush tops with a little extra milk.
5 Bake for about 15 minutes or until browned and scones sound hollow when tapped firmly on the top with fingers.

preparation 20 minutes
cooking time 15 minutes
makes 16
per scone 2.9g fat 527kj (126 cal)

PUMPKIN SCONES

The most popular American bread at breakfast is the 'biscuit'. Although recipes vary slightly from State to State, they are often made with buttermilk and use baking powder or soda as a leavening agent rather than yeast. They are closely related to the British scone, so these pumpkin scones make a delicious alternative.

CHEESE, CORN & BACON MUFFINS

Hearty soups

FARMHOUSE CHICKEN SOUP

1.5kg whole chicken
1 small brown onion (80g), halved
2 litres (8 cups) water
5 black peppercorns
2 bay leaves
20g butter
2 trimmed celery stalks (200g), sliced thinly
2 medium carrots (240g), cut into 1cm pieces
1 large potato (300g), cut into 1cm pieces
150g mangetout, trimmed, chopped coarsely
3 spring onions, sliced thinly
310g can corn kernels, drained

1 Place chicken, brown onion, the water, peppercorns and bay leaves in large saucepan; bring to the boil. Reduce heat; simmer, covered, 2 hours.
2 Remove chicken from pan. Strain broth through colander into large bowl; discard solids. Allow broth to cool, cover; refrigerate overnight. When chicken is cool enough to handle, remove and discard skin and bones. Shred meat coarsely; cover, refrigerate overnight.
3 Heat butter in same cleaned pan; cook celery, carrot and potato, stirring, until onion softens. Skim and discard fat from surface of broth. Add to pan; bring to the boil. Reduce heat; simmer, covered, about 10 minutes or until vegetables are just tender.
4 Add mangetout, spring onion, corn and reserved chicken to soup; cook, covered, 5 minutes or until heated through.

preparation time 25 minutes (plus refrigeration)
cooking time 2 hours 15 minutes
serves 6
per serving 9.2g fat; 1183kj (283 cal)

CREAM OF PUMPKIN SOUP

40g butter
1 large onion (200g), chopped coarsely
3 bacon rashers (210g), chopped coarsely
1.5kg pumpkin (or butternut squash), chopped coarsely
2 large potatoes (600g), chopped coarsely
1.25 litres (5 cups) chicken stock
½ cup (125ml) double cream

1 Melt butter in large saucepan; cook onion and bacon, stirring, until onion softens. Stir in pumpkin and potato.
2 Stir in stock, bring to the boil; simmer, uncovered, about 20 minutes or until pumpkin is soft.
3 Blend or process soup, in batches, until smooth. Return soup to same cleaned pan, add cream; stir until heated through.

preparation time 20 minutes
cooking time 20 minutes
serves 6
per serving 20.9g fat; 1555kj (372 cal)
tip You can use butternut squash in this recipe, which is available all year round.

CREAM OF PUMPKIN SOUP

FARMHOUSE CHICKEN SOUP

Beef dishes

MEATLOAF

1 small red pepper (150g)
400g minced beef
150g sausagemeat
1 medium onion (150g), chopped finely
2 cloves garlic, crushed
¼ cup (25g) packaged breadcrumbs
1 egg, beaten lightly
½ cup (80g) coarsely chopped pitted green olives
¼ cup coarsely chopped fresh basil
1 tablespoon coarsely chopped fresh oregano
8 bacon rashers (560g), rind removed, sliced thickly lengthways

glaze
¼ cup (60ml) water
1 tablespoon tomato paste
1 tablespoon red wine vinegar
2 tablespoons brown sugar

1 Quarter pepper; discard seeds and membrane. Roast under grill or in very hot oven, skin-side up, until skin blisters and blackens. Cover pepper pieces with plastic or paper for 5 minutes. Peel away skin; slice flesh thinly.
2 Preheat oven to moderate (180°C/160°C fan-assisted). Line 8cm x 25cm cake tin with cling film. Lightly oil 25cm x 30cm swiss roll tin.
3 Using hand, combine mince, sausagemeat, onion, garlic, breadcrumbs, egg, olives and herbs in large bowl. Press half of the meatloaf mixture into cake tin. Lay pepper strips over top, leaving 1cm border; press remaining meatloaf mixture over pepper.
4 Turn cake tin onto swiss roll tin; remove cling from meatloaf. Cover top and sides of meatloaf with bacon, overlapping slices. Bake, uncovered, 15 minutes.
5 Meanwhile, make glaze.
6 Pour off any excess fat from meatloaf, brush with glaze; bake, uncovered, 25 minutes or until meatloaf is cooked through. Stand 10 minutes before serving.

glaze Combine ingredients in small saucepan; bring to a boil. Reduce heat; simmer, uncovered, 5 minutes.

preparation time 20 minutes
cooking time 50 minutes
serves 4
per serving 35.3g fat; 2633kj (630 cal)
tip Cold meatloaf makes a delicious sandwich filling on sourdough bread. Serve with melted cheese, mixed salad leaves and a chunky beetroot relish.

CORNED BEEF

Corned beef – a piece of beef cured or pickled in brine – is often associated with St Patrick's Day in America, when many Irish Americans eat a traditional meal of corned beef and cabbage. A similar dish is the New England boiled dinner, which consists of corned beef, cabbage and root vegetables.

FAMILY BEEF STEW

CORNED BEEF WITH PARSLEY SAUCE

1.5kg whole piece beef corned silverside
2 bay leaves
6 black peppercorns
1 large onion (200g), quartered
1 large carrot (180g), chopped coarsely
1 tablespoon brown malt vinegar
¼ cup (50g) firmly packed brown sugar

parsley sauce
30g butter
¼ cup (35g) plain flour
2½ cups (625ml) milk
⅓ cup (40g) grated cheddar cheese
⅓ cup finely chopped fresh flat-leaf parsley
1 tablespoon american mustard

1 Place beef, bay leaves, peppercorns, onion, carrot, vinegar and half of the sugar in large pan. Add enough water to just cover beef; simmer, covered, about 2 hours or until beef is tender. Cool beef 1 hour in liquid in pan.
2 Remove beef from pan; discard liquid. Sprinkle sheet of foil with remaining sugar, wrap beef in foil; stand 20 minutes.
3 Make parsley sauce.
4 Serve sliced beef with parsley sauce.

parsley sauce Melt butter in small sauce-pan, add flour; cook, stirring, until bubbling. Gradually stir in milk; cook, stirring, until sauce boils and thickens. Remove from heat; stir in cheese, parsley and mustard.

preparation time 30 minutes (plus standing and cooling time)
cooking time 2 hours
serves 4
per serving 35.8g fat; 3520kj (842 cal)

FAMILY BEEF STEW

2 tablespoons vegetable oil
2kg beef chuck steak, chopped coarsely
2 medium onions (300g), sliced thinly
2 medium carrots (240g), sliced thickly
3 cloves garlic, crushed
¼ cup finely chopped fresh flat-leaf parsley
¼ cup (70g) tomato paste
2 teaspoons american mustard
1 cup (250ml) dry red wine
½ cup (125ml) beef stock

1 Preheat oven to 150°C/130°C fan-assisted.
2 Heat oil in 2.5 litre (10-cup) flameproof casserole dish; cook beef, in batches, until browned.
3 Cook onion, carrot and garlic in same dish, stirring over heat, until onion is soft.
4 Return beef to dish; stir in parsley, paste, mustard, wine and stock. Cook, covered, in oven about 1¾ hours or until beef is tender. Serve stew with mash (see page 33).

preparation time 15 minutes
cooking time 2 hours 15 minutes
serves 6
per serving 21.4g fat; 2203kJ (527 cal)

Lamb dishes

LAMB POT ROAST

2 x 1kg boned rolled lamb shoulders
2 cloves garlic, crushed
2 fresh rosemary sprigs
1 teaspoon coarsely chopped fresh thyme
1 teaspoon grated orange rind
1 cup (250ml) dry red wine
1 teaspoon olive oil
4 bacon rashers (285g), chopped coarsely
370g spring onions, trimmed
1 tablespoon chicken stock powder
12 baby new potatoes (480g)
2 medium carrots (240g), halved
2 teaspoons cornflour
1 tablespoon water

MAPLE SYRUP-GLAZED LAMB SHANKS

1 Combine lamb, garlic, herbs, rind and wine in large bowl; cover, refrigerate several hours or overnight.
2 Remove lamb from marinade; reserve marinade. Pat lamb dry with absorbent paper; brush with oil.
3 Heat 3 litre (12-cup) deep, flameproof casserole dish; cook lamb until browned all over. Remove from dish. Add bacon and onion to dish; cook, stirring, until onion is browned lightly.
4 Return lamb to dish. Add reserved marinade and stock powder; cook, covered in moderate oven 45 minutes.
5 Add potatoes and carrot; cook, covered, about 1 hour or until lamb and vegetables are tender. Remove lamb and vegetables from dish.

6 Discard all but 2 cups (500ml) of the cooking liquid. Add blended cornflour and water to dish. Stir in cooking liquid; stir over heat until mixture boils and thickens slightly.
7 Serve sliced lamb accompanied by vegetables and sauce.

preparation time 20 minutes
(plus marinating time)
cooking time 2 hours
serves 8
per serving 16.7g fat; 1858kJ (444 cal)
tips Pot roast can be made a day ahead and refrigerated, covered. Recipe suitable to freeze; thicken with cornflour just before serving.

MAPLE SYRUP-GLAZED LAMB SHANKS

⅓ cup (80ml) pure maple syrup
1 cup (250ml) chicken stock
1 tablespoon american mustard
1½ cups (375ml) orange juice
8 extra-trimmed lamb shanks (2kg)

1 Combine syrup, stock, mustard and juice in large deep flameproof casserole dish, add lamb; toss lamb to coat in syrup mixture. Bring to the boil then cover tightly. Reduce heat; cook lamb, turning every 20 minutes, about 2 hours or until lamb is tender.
2 Serve lamb with roast potatoes and wilted baby spinach leaves, if desired.

preparation time 10 minutes
cooking time 2 hours
serves 4
per serving 5.2g fat; 1668kJ (399 cal)

Pork dishes

PORK & BEANS

3 cloves garlic, crushed
½ teaspoon freshly ground black pepper
1.8kg pork neck
1 tablespoon olive oil
3 rindless bacon rashers (195g),
chopped finely
2 medium onions (300g), sliced thinly
2 teaspoons caraway seeds
375ml can beer
1 cup (200g) dried haricot beans
1½ cups (375ml) chicken stock
¼ small (300g) white cabbage, shredded
finely

1 Rub combined garlic and pepper all over
pork. Secure pork with string at 2cm intervals
to make an even shape.
2 Heat oil in large flameproof casserole
dish; cook pork until browned all over.
Remove from dish.
3 Cook bacon, onion and seeds in same
dish, stirring, until onion is soft and bacon
browned lightly.
4 Return pork to dish with beer, beans and
stock; simmer, covered, about 2 hours or
until beans and pork are tender. Remove pork
from dish. Add cabbage; cook, stirring, until
just wilted.

preparation time 20 minutes
cooking time 2 hours 20 minutes
serves 8
per serving 24.4g fat; 2261kJ (541 cal)

MAPLE-SYRUP-FLAVOURED PORK BELLY WITH PECANS

1kg boneless pork belly, cut into four pieces
1 cup (250ml) pure maple syrup
3 cups (750ml) chicken stock
1 cinnamon stick
2 chillies
6 whole cloves
2 cloves garlic, crushed
½ cup (125ml) soy sauce
½ cup (125ml) orange juice
1 tablespoon olive oil
750g swiss chard, trimmed, sliced thinly
½ cup (60g) coarsely chopped roasted pecans

1 Combine pork, syrup, stock, cinnamon,
chillies, cloves, garlic and soy in large pan;
bring to the boil. Reduce heat; simmer,
covered, about 1½ hours or until pork is
tender, turning pork every 30 minutes.
Remove pork; cover to keep warm.
2 Stir juice into braising liquid; bring to the
boil. Reduce heat; simmer, uncovered, about
5 minutes or until sauce thickens slightly.
Strain sauce into small bowl.
3 Meanwhile, heat oil in large pan; cook
chard, stirring, about 5 minutes until wilted.
4 Cut each pork piece into quarters. Divide
chard among plates; top with pork, drizzle
with sauce then sprinkle with nuts. Serve
with mashed potato, if desired.

preparation time 20 minutes
cooking time 1 hour 50 minutes
serves 4
per serving 67.2g fat; 4080kJ (976 cal)

MAPLE-SYRUP-FLAVOURED PORK BELLY WITH PECANS

PORK & BEANS

Poultry

GLAZED TURKEY WITH CORNBREAD STUFFING

4kg turkey
20g butter
6 shallots (150g)
1 large apple (200g), cut into 6 wedges
1 tablespoon fresh sage leaves
20 black peppercorns
2 cups (500ml) water
1 cup (250ml) chicken stock
½ cup (125ml) brandy
50g butter, melted
½ cup (125ml) molasses
2 tablespoons plain flour

macerated fruit
¼ cup (35g) coarsely chopped dried apricots
¼ cup (35g) currants
⅓ cup (80ml) brandy

1 Two days before, make macerated fruit.
2 On the day you want to roast the turkey, preheat oven to 180°C/160°C fan-assisted. Discard neck from turkey. Rinse turkey under cold water; pat dry inside and out with absorbent paper.
3 Heat butter in large saucepan; cook whole shallots and apple, stirring, until browned lightly. Cool 10 minutes; stir in sage and peppercorns. Tuck wings under turkey, fill large cavity loosely with stuffing; tie legs together with kitchen string.
4 Place turkey on oiled wire rack in large shallow flameproof baking dish; pour the water, stock and brandy into dish. Brush turkey all over with melted butter; cover dish tightly with two layers of greased foil. Roast 2 hours 10 minutes.
5 Meanwhile, make cornbread stuffing.
6 Uncover turkey; brush with half of the molasses. Roast, uncovered, about 20 minutes or until browned all over and cooked through, brushing frequently with remaining molasses. Remove turkey from dish, cover turkey; stand 20 minutes.
7 Pour juice from dish into large jug; skim 1 tablespoon of the fat from juice, return to same dish. Skim and discard remaining fat from juice. Add flour to dish; cook, stirring, until mixture bubbles and is well browned. Gradually stir in juice; bring to a boil, stirring, until gravy boils and thickens. Strain gravy into same jug; serve turkey with cornbread stuffing and gravy.

macerated fruit Combine ingredients in small glass jar, cover; stand at room temperature for two days.

preparation time 1 hour 30 minutes
cooking time 3 hours 30 minutes
(plus cooling and standing time)
serves 10
per serving 45.5g fat; 3461kj (828 cal)
tip To test if turkey is cooked, insert a skewer sideways into the thickest part of the thigh then remove and press the flesh to release the juices. If the juice runs clear, the turkey is cooked. Alternatively, insert a meat thermometer into the thickest part of the turkey thigh, without touching the bone; it should reach 90°C.

Cornbread stuffing

350g chorizo, chopped finely
1 medium onion (150g), chopped coarsely
2 shallots (50g), chopped coarsely
1 large apple (200g), chopped coarsely
1 tablespoon sage leaves, torn
2 cups (500ml) apple juice
3½ cups (340g) coarsely chopped stale cornbread (see page 78)

1 Line 7cm x 21cm loaf tin with baking parchment, extending it 5cm over long sides.

2 Cook chorizo in large frying pan, stirring, until browned lightly. Add onion and shallot; cook, stirring, until onion softens. Add apple; cook, stirring, until browned lightly. Remove from heat; stir in sage, juice, cornbread and ⅔ cup (180g) macerated fruit.

3 Place stuffing in prepared tin in oven with turkey; cook, uncovered, during last 30 minutes of turkey roasting time.

CHICKEN POT ROAST

HOMESTEAD CHICKEN PIE

60g butter
1 medium leek (350g), sliced thickly
⅓ cup (50g) plain flour
¾ cup (180ml) milk
1 cup (250ml) chicken stock
3 cups (480g) coarsely chopped cooked
chicken
1 cup (85g) chopped broccoli
1 small red pepper (150g), chopped finely
310g can corn kernels, drained
¼ cup coarsely chopped flat-leaf parsley
2 sheets ready-rolled puff pastry
1 egg

1 Melt butter in medium saucepan; cook leek, stirring, about 1 minute or until leek is soft. Add flour; cook, stirring, until mixture bubbles. Remove from heat, gradually stir in milk and stock; cook, stirring, over heat until mixture boils and thickens. Remove from heat; stir in chicken, broccoli, pepper, corn and parsley.
2 Preheat oven to 200°C/180°C fan-assisted.
3 Spoon filling into 23cm pie dish. Cut 3cm wide strips from one sheet of pastry and place them around the lip of dish. Brush strips lightly with egg. Place second sheet of pastry over filling and lip to cover dish. Trim edge, scallop edge firmly to seal, decorate with pastry scraps, if desired. Brush top of pastry with egg.
4 Bake pie, uncovered, about 10 minutes; reduce oven temperature to 180°C/160°C fan-assisted, bake further 20 minutes or until pastry is brown.
preparation time 30 minutes
cooking time 45 minutes
serves 6
per serving 29.4g fat; 2291kJ (548 cal)

CHICKEN POT ROAST WITH MUSTARD CREAM SAUCE

1.6kg chicken
1 tablespoon olive oil
12 shallots (300g), halved
20 baby carrots (400g), trimmed
3 small parsnips (360g), chopped coarsely
1 cup (250ml) dry white wine
2 cups (500ml) chicken stock
2 bay leaves
200g chestnut mushrooms
2 tablespoons double cream
2 tablespoons wholegrain mustard

1 Preheat oven to 200°C/180°C fan-assisted.
2 Wash chicken under cold water; pat dry inside and out with absorbent paper.
3 Heat oil in large flameproof casserole dish; cook chicken until browned all over. Remove chicken. Cook shallots, carrots and parsnip in same dish, stirring, about 5 minutes or until vegetables are browned lightly.
4 Return chicken to dish with wine, stock and bay leaves; bring to a boil. Cook, covered, in oven 30 minutes. Uncover; cook about 30 minutes or until chicken is cooked through. Add mushrooms; cook, uncovered, about 10 minutes or until mushrooms are tender.
5 Remove chicken and vegetables from dish; cover to keep warm. Add cream and mustard to dish; bring to a boil. Boil, uncovered, about 5 minutes or until sauce thickens slightly.
6 Serve chicken with vegetables and mustard cream sauce.
preparation time 25 minutes
cooking time 1 hour 50 minutes
serves 4
per serving 42.2g fat; 2859kJ (684 cal)

Side dishes

BABY CARROTS WITH ORANGE MAPLE SYRUP

1.6kg baby carrots
30g butter
2 teaspoons finely grated orange rind
2 tablespoons orange juice
2 tablespoons maple syrup

1 Boil, steam or microwave carrots until just tender.
2 Melt butter in large frying pan; stir rind, juice and syrup in pan until mixture boils. Reduce heat; simmer, uncovered, until syrup mixture thickens slightly. Add drained carrots to pan, stirring gently to coat in orange maple syrup.

preparation time 35 minutes
cooking time 20 minutes
serves 8
per serving 3.3g fat; 426kj (102 cal)

BUTTERNUT SQUASH WITH WALNUT DRESSING

800g butternut squash, sliced thickly

walnut dressing
½ cup (50g) toasted chopped walnuts
¼ cup (60ml) lemon juice
½ cup (125ml) olive oil
1 tablespoon american mustard
2 tablespoons finely chopped fresh chives

1 Cook squash on heated oiled barbecue or roast in a hot oven until browned all over and tender.
2 Serve squash drizzled with walnut dressing.

walnut dressing Combine ingredients in screw-top jar; shake well.

preparation time 15 minutes
cooking time 15 minutes
serves 4
per serving 37.9g fat; 1695kJ (405 cal)

LEMON & GARLIC CORN COBS

6 trimmed corn cobs (1.5kg)
2 teaspoons shredded lemon rind
1 tablespoon wholegrain mustard
2 cloves garlic, crushed
2 tablespoons coarsely chopped chives
⅓ cup (80ml) lemon juice
⅓ cup (80ml) groundnut oil

1 Cook corn on heated oiled barbecue, uncovered, until browned all over.
2 Serve corn drizzled with combined remaining ingredients.

preparation time 15 minutes
cooking time 15 minutes
serves 6
per serving 15.1g fat; 1427kJ (341 cal)

BABY CARROTS WITH
ORANGE MAPLE SYRUP

LEMON & GARLIC CORN COBS

CREAMY MASHED POTATO

Native to South America, the potato was brought back to Europe by Spanish conquistadors in the 16th century. It eventually made its way back across the Atlantic to North America where it soon became a popular staple of the American diet.

CREAMY MASHED POTATO

1kg floury potatoes, peeled, cut into
3cm pieces
40g butter, softened
¾ cup (180ml) hot milk

1 Place potato in medium saucepan with
enough cold water to barely cover the potato.
Boil, uncovered, over medium heat about
15 minutes or until potato is tender. Drain.
2 Using a potato masher or large fork, mash
the potato. Stir butter and hot milk into
potato, folding gently until mash is smooth
and fluffy.

preparation time 10 minutes
cooking time 20 minutes
serves 4
per serving 10.2g fat; 991kJ (237 cal)
tip For really smooth mash, push the potato
through a fine sieve with the back of a
wooden spoon, or use a potato ricer.

CELERIAC MASH

800g floury potatoes, peeled, chopped
coarsely
1kg celeriac, peeled, chopped coarsely
½ cup (125ml) hot cream
60g butter, softened

1 Boil, steam or microwave potato and
celeriac, separately, until tender; drain.
2 Mash potato and celeriac in large bowl;
stir in cream and butter until combined.

preparation time 10 minutes
cooking time 25 minutes
serves 4
per serving 26.5g fat; 1697kJ (406 cal)

SWEET POTATO MASH

500g floury potatoes, peeled, chopped
coarsely
500g sweet potatoes, peeled, chopped
coarsely
¼ cup (60ml) hot chicken stock
40g butter, melted

1 Boil, steam or microwave potato and sweet
potatoes, together, until tender; drain.
2 Mash potato and sweet potatoes in large
bowl; stir in stock and butter.

preparation time 10 minutes
cooking time 20 minutes
serves 4
per serving 8.5g fat; 903kJ (216 cal)

PEA MASH

1kg floury potatoes, peeled, coarsely
chopped
1½ cups (180g) frozen peas
¾ cup (180ml) hot milk
50g butter, softened

1 Boil, steam or microwave potato and peas,
separately, until tender; drain.
2 Mash potato in large bowl; stir in milk and
butter.
3 Using fork, mash peas in small bowl; stir
into potato mixture until combined.

preparation time 10 minutes
cooking time 20 minutes
serves 4
per serving 12.4g fat; 1212kJ (290 cal)

Home-baked pies

APRICOT & ALMOND APPLE PIE

10 medium granny smith apples (1.5kg),
peeled, cored, sliced thickly
½ cup (125ml) water
1 tablespoon caster sugar
⅔ cup (220g) apricot jam
1 teaspoon finely grated lemon rind
¼ cup (20g) flaked almonds

pastry
1 cup (150g) plain flour
½ cup (75g) self-raising flour
¼ cup (35g) cornflour
¼ cup (30g) custard powder
1 tablespoon caster sugar
100g chilled butter, chopped coarsely
1 egg, separated
¼ cup (60ml) iced water, approximately

1 Make pastry.
2 Meanwhile, combine apple and the water in large pan; bring to the boil. Reduce heat; simmer, covered, 10 minutes or until apples soften. Drain well; transfer to a bowl, stir in sugar, jam and rind. Cool.
3 Preheat oven to 220°C/200°C fan-assisted. Grease deep 25cm pie dish.
4 Roll two-thirds of the pastry between sheets of baking parchment until large enough to line dish. Lift pastry into dish, smooth over base and side. Brush all over with egg white. Spoon apple mixture into dish; brush edge with egg white.
5 Roll out remaining pastry. Place over filling; press edges to seal. Brush pastry with egg white; sprinkle with caster sugar and nuts.

6 Bake pie 20 minutes. Reduce oven temperature to 180°C/160°C fan-assisted; bake 25 minutes.

pastry Process flours, custard powder, sugar and butter until crumbly. Add egg yolk and enough of the water to process until ingredients come together. Knead dough on floured surface until smooth. Enclose in cling film; refrigerate 30 minutes.

preparation time 45 minutes
(plus chilling time)
cooking time 1 hour 10 minutes
serves 8

SPICED HARVEST PIE

In the past a pie always had two crusts, top and bottom. Then all the exceptions started, for example lemon meringue pie certainly has a topping but it's not pastry. Spiced Harvest Pie however, only has pastry on top. If you can, use an old-fashioned enamel dish — they transfer heat really fast so they're great for pastry baking.

SPICED HARVEST PIE

2 x 825g cans dark plums in light syrup
2 cups (300g) dried apricots
1 cinnamon stick
3 cloves
½ teaspoon mixed spice
½ teaspoon ground ginger
1 teaspoon finely grated orange rind
2 sheets ready-rolled puff pastry
1 egg, beaten lightly
icing sugar, for dusting

1 Preheat oven to moderately hot (200°C/180°C fan-assisted). Grease 26cm pie dish or deep 1.25 litre (5-cup) rectangular dish.
2 Drain plums; reserve 1 cup (250ml) of the syrup. Halve plums, discard stones; place plums in prepared dish.
3 Combine reserved syrup, apricots, cinnamon, cloves, mixed spice, ginger and orange rind in medium saucepan; simmer, uncovered, until liquid is reduced to ½ cup (125ml). Remove and discard cinnamon stick and cloves; cool to room temperature. Pour mixture over plums.
4 Cut pastry into 2.5cm strips. Brush edge of dish with a little of the egg; press pastry strips around edge of dish. Twist remaining strips, place over filling in a lattice pattern; trim ends, brush top with remaining egg.
5 Bake, uncovered, 40 minutes or until pastry is browned lightly.
6 Dust pie generously with icing sugar and serve with cream.

preparation time 30 minutes
cooking time 45 minutes (plus cooling time)
serves 8

BLUEBERRY & APPLE PIES

1 cup (150g) plain flour
⅓ cup (55g) icing sugar
90g chilled butter, chopped coarsely
1 egg yolk
3 teaspoons iced water, approximately
2 tablespoons roasted slivered almonds

filling
1 small apple (130g), grated coarsely
½ cup (75g) frozen blueberries
1 teaspoon ground cinnamon
2 teaspoons finely grated lemon rind

1 Preheat oven to 180°C/160°C fan-assisted. Grease two 12-hole (20ml) mini muffin pans.
2 Pulse flour, sugar and butter in food processor until crumbly. Add egg yolk and enough of the water to process until ingredients come together.
3 Shape one-quarter of the dough into thick sausage. Enclose in cling film; freeze 45 minutes.
4 Meanwhile, roll remaining dough to 4mm thickness, cut out 24 x 6cm rounds; press rounds into pan holes. Refrigerate 15 minutes.
5 Make filling; divide filling among pastry cases. Coarsely grate frozen dough evenly over filling; sprinkle with nuts.
6 Bake pies about 20 minutes. Stand pies in pans 5 minutes; transfer to wire rack to cool.

preparation time 30 minutes
(plus freezing and refrigeration times)
cooking time 20 minutes
makes 24

A cool drink on the porch...

HOMEMADE LEMONADE

4 medium lemons (560g)
4 cups (880g) caster sugar
2 cups (500ml) water
5 litres (20 cups) mineral water

1 Remove rind from lemons using a
vegetable peeler, avoiding white pith; reserve
lemons. Combine rind, sugar and the water
in large saucepan; stir over low heat, without
boiling, until sugar is dissolved. Bring to a
boil, simmer, uncovered, without stirring,
about 10 minutes or until syrup is thickened
slightly; cool.
2 Squeeze juice from lemons – you will need
1 cup (250ml) lemon juice. Add juice to syrup,
strain into jug; cover, keep refrigerated.
3 Just before serving, add four parts mineral
water to one part lemonade, or to taste.

preparation time 10 minutes
(plus refrigeration time)
makes 6.25 litres (25 cups) diluted lemonade
or 1.25 litres (5 cups) undiluted lemonade
per 250ml (diluted) 0g fat; 293kJ (70 cal)

PINK LIMEADE

1 cup (250ml) lime juice (approx. 8 limes)
½ cup (125ml) vodka
2½ cups (625ml) water
1 litre (4 cups) cranberry juice

1 Combine ingredients in large jug.
2 Cover; refrigerate until chilled.

preparation time 10 minutes
(plus refrigeration time)
makes 2 litres
per 250ml 0.1g fat; 535kJ (128 cal)

PEACH ICED TEA

1 large orange (300g)
½ cup (125ml) water
½ cup (110g) caster sugar
1.25 litres (5 cups) boiling water
3 black tea bags
3 peach-flavoured herbal infusion bags
1⅔ cups (400ml) peach nectar
¼ cup loosely packed fresh mint leaves
1½ cups ice cubes

1 Peel rind thinly from half the orange. Peel
off white pith, cut orange into thin slices.
2 Place the water and sugar in small
saucepan; stir over low heat, without boiling,
until sugar dissolves. Add rind; simmer,
uncovered, without stirring, about 5 minutes
or until thickened slightly. Discard rind, cool
15 minutes. Cover; refrigerate until required.
3 Pour boiling water in large heatproof jug,
add black tea and peach tea bags; infuse for
5 minutes. Remove tea bags; cool 10 minutes.
Cover; refrigerate until chilled.
4 Place sugar syrup, tea, orange slices, nectar,
mint and ice in large jug; stir to combine.

preparation time 10 minutes
(plus refrigeration time)
serves 8
per serving 0.2g fat; 418kj (100 cal)

HOMEMADE LEMONADE

PINK LIMEADE

Ranch-style breakfast

EGGS RANCHEROS

1 tablespoon olive oil
1 small red onion (100g), chopped finely
4 medium tomatoes (600g), chopped coarsely
2 tablespoons water
1 tablespoon red wine vinegar
1 medium red pepper (200g), chopped finely
4 eggs
4 corn tortillas

1 Heat oil in large frying pan; cook onion, stirring, until softened. Add tomato, the water and vinegar. Bring to a boil then reduce heat; simmer, uncovered, 15 minutes, stirring occasionally. Add pepper; cook, uncovered, 5 minutes.
2 Using large shallow mixing spoon, press four shallow depressions into tomato mixture. Working quickly, break eggs, one at a time, into cup, sliding each egg into one of the hollows in tomato mixture. Cover pan; cook over low heat, about 5 minutes or until eggs are just set.
3 Divide warmed tortillas among plates. Use egg slide to carefully lift egg and tomato mixture onto each tortilla.

preparation time 10 minutes
cooking time 30 minutes
serves 4
per serving 11.2g fat; 1087kJ (206 cal)

CORN & COURGETTE FRITTERS WITH AVOCADO SALSA

50g butter, melted
½ cup (125ml) milk
¾ cup (110g) plain flour
2 eggs, beaten lightly
210g can creamed corn
2 medium courgettes (240g), grated coarsely
vegetable oil, for shallow-frying

avocado salsa
3 medium plum tomatoes (225g), chopped coarsely
2 medium avocados (500g), chopped coarsely
1 small red onion (100g), chopped coarsely
2 tablespoons lime juice
2 tablespoons finely chopped fresh coriander

1 Make salsa.
2 Combine butter, milk, flour and egg in medium bowl; whisk until smooth. Add corn and courgettes; mix well.
3 Heat oil in medium frying pan; cook heaped tablespoons of batter about 2 minutes each side or until browned both sides and cooked through. Drain on absorbent paper. Serve warm with salsa.

avocado salsa Combine all ingredients together in small bowl.

preparation time 20 minutes
cooking time 20 minutes
serves 4
per serving 54.4g fat; 2700kJ (646 cal)

EGGS RANCHEROS

CORN & COURGETTE FRITTERS

Cheesy sourdough

To accompany your soup, cut a loaf of sourdough bread into 3cm slices. Combine 2 tablespoons olive oil and 2 teaspoons finely grated parmesan in large bowl; add bread, turn to coat well. Place slices on oven tray and toast in a preheated oven (180°C/160°C fan-assisted), both sides, about 15 minutes.

Spicy soups

TORTILLA LIME SOUP

1 medium white onion (150g), chopped
2 cloves garlic, quartered
1 fresh long red chilli, chopped coarsely
4 medium tomatoes (600g), peeled,
quartered
1 tablespoon groundnut oil
¼ teaspoon ground allspice
1½ cups (375ml) chicken stock
1.25 litres (5 cups) water
2 teaspoons grated lime rind
¼ cup (60ml) lime juice
¼ cup (70g) tomato paste
⅓ cup (80ml) groundnut oil, extra
6 corn tortillas, cut into 2cm-wide strips
1 medium avocado (250g), chopped finely
2 spring onions, chopped finely
¼ cup coarsely chopped fresh coriander

1 Blend or process white onion, garlic, chilli
and tomato until pureed.
2 Heat oil in large saucepan; cook tomato
mixture and allspice, stirring, until fragrant.
3 Add stock, water, rind, juice and paste. Bring
to a boil then reduce heat; simmer, uncovered,
15 minutes or until mixture thickens.
4 Meanwhile, heat extra oil in frying pan;
cook tortilla strips in batches, until golden.
Drain on kitchen paper. Divide tortillas among
bowls; ladle soup over. Top with combined
avocado, spring onion and coriander.

preparation time 20 minutes
cooking time 25 minutes
serves 4
per serving 26g fat; 1777kJ (425 cal)

TOMATO & PEPPER SOUP

2 large red peppers (700g)
5 large vine-ripened tomatoes (1.2kg), halved
1 tablespoon olive oil
1 medium onion (150g), chopped coarsely
2 cloves garlic, crushed
4 fresh long red chillies, chopped coarsely
2 cups (500ml) water
2 cups (500ml) vegetable stock
cooking-oil spray
2 tablespoons soured cream
2 tablespoons finely chopped fresh chives

1 Preheat oven to 240°C (220°C fan-assisted).
2 Quarter peppers, discard seeds and
membranes. Roast peppers, skin-side up, and
tomato, cut-side up, on lightly oiled oven
trays, uncovered, about 15 minutes or until
pepper skin blisters and blackens and tomato
softens. Cover peppers with plastic for
5 minutes; peel away skin, cover to keep
warm. Cool tomato 5 minutes; peel off skin.
3 Heat oil in large pan; cook onion, garlic
and chilli, stirring, until onion softens. Add
pepper and tomato; cook, stirring, 5 minutes.
Add the water and stock. Bring to a boil then
reduce heat; simmer, uncovered, 10 minutes.
4 Blend or process tomato mixture, in
batches, until smooth. Pass through fine sieve
into large saucepan; discard solids.
5 Divide soup among serving bowls; top with
soured cream and chives.

preparation time 20 minutes
cooking time 35 minutes
serves 4
per serving 9.7g fat; 807kJ (193 cal)

Salsas & dips

CHILE CON QUESO

2 teaspoons vegetable oil
½ small green pepper (75g), chopped finely
½ small onion (40g), chopped finely
1 tablespoon pickled jalapeño chillies,
chopped finely
1 clove garlic, crushed
½ x 400g can undrained chopped tomatoes
250g cream cheese, softened

1 Heat oil in medium saucepan; cook pepper,
onion, chilli and garlic, stirring, until onion
softens. Add tomato; cook, stirring, 2 minutes.
2 Add cheese; whisk until cheese melts and
dip is smooth. Serve hot with corn chips.

preparation time 10 minutes
cooking time 10 minutes
makes 2 cups
per tablespoon 3.9g fat; 174kJ (42 cal)

MANGO & AVOCADO SALSA

1 medium mango (430g), chopped coarsely
1 large avocado (320g), chopped coarsely
1 small red onion (100g), chopped finely
1 small red pepper (150g), chopped finely
1 fresh small red chilli, chopped finely
2 tablespoons lime juice

1 Combine ingredients in medium bowl.

preparation time 15 minutes
makes 2½ cups
per tablespoon 1.7g fat; 100kJ (24 cal)

GUACAMOLE

2 medium avocados (500g), mashed
½ small red onion (50g), chopped finely
1 plum tomato (75g), deseeded, chopped finely
1 tablespoon lime juice
¼ cup coarsely chopped fresh coriander

1 Combine ingredients in medium bowl.

preparation time 10 minutes
makes 2½ cups
per tablespoon 4g fat; 157kJ (38 cal)

CORN & COURGETTE SALSA

2 corn cobs (800g), trimmed
100g baby courgettes, halved lengthways
2 large avocados (640g), chopped coarsely
200g cherry tomatoes, halved
1 medium red onion (170g), sliced thickly
¼ cup coarsely chopped fresh coriander
1 tablespoon sweet chilli sauce
⅓ cup (80ml) lime juice
2 fresh small red chillies, sliced thinly

1 Cook corn and courgettes under preheated
grill until tender and browned lightly. Using
sharp knife, remove kernels from cobs.
2 Combine corn and courgettes in large bowl
with avocado, tomato, onion and coriander.
Add remaining ingredients; toss gently.

preparation time 20 minutes
cooking time 10 minutes
makes 7 cups
per tablespoon 1.3g.fat; 84kJ (20 cal)

CORN & COURGETTE SALSA

The word 'salsa' can refer to any type of sauce, but in Tex-Mex cuisine it usually refers to the spicy, often tomato-based sauce made from chopped, diced or grated vegetables, fruit, spices and seasonings. Salsa can be used as an accompaniment to meat and fish dishes, as a filling for tortillas or as a dip.

GUACAMOLE

Snacks

EMPANADAS

400g can tomatoes
1 tablespoon olive oil
1 medium onion (150g), chopped finely
1 clove garlic, crushed
1 teaspoon freshly ground black pepper
½ teaspoon ground cinnamon
½ teaspoon ground cloves
600g minced beef
¼ cup (40g) raisins, chopped coarsely
1 tablespoon cider vinegar
¼ cup (35g) toasted slivered almonds
2 x 800g packets ready-rolled quiche pastry
1 egg, beaten lightly
vegetable oil, for deep-frying

1 Blend or process undrained tomatoes until smooth; reserve.
2 Heat olive oil in large heavy-based pan; cook onion, garlic and spices, stirring, until onion is soft. Add beef; cook, stirring, until changed in colour. Drain away excess fat. Stir in reserved tomato, raisins and vinegar; simmer, uncovered, about 20 minutes or until filling mixture thickens. Stir in nuts.
3 Cut 9cm rounds from each pastry sheet (you will get 32 rounds). Place a level tablespoon of the beef mixture in centre of each round; brush edge lightly with egg. Fold pastry over to enclose filling; press edges together to seal.
4 Heat vegetable oil in large deep-frying pan. Deep-fry empanadas until crisp and browned lightly; drain on absorbent paper. Serve immediately with a dollop of soured cream or salsa, if desired.

preparation time 40 minutes
cooking time 45 minutes
serves 8
per serving 26g fat; 1664kJ (398 cal)
tip For a lower-fat version, empanadas can be baked, uncovered, in a preheated hot oven about 25 minutes or until browned.

BEAN & TOMATO TOSTADA WEDGES

1 tablespoon olive oil
1 small onion (80g), chopped finely
425g can mexican-style beans, drained
½ cup (130g) bottled tomato salsa
⅓ cup (80g) soured cream
3 large flour tortillas, cut into wedges
½ cup (60g) coarsely grated cheddar cheese

1 Preheat oven to hot (220°C/200°C fan-assisted).
2 Heat oil in small frying pan; cook onion, stirring, until softened. Blend or process onion with beans until almost smooth; return to same pan. Add salsa and soured cream; stir until heated through. Place tortilla triangles onto lightly oiled oven trays; top with bean mixture and cheese.
3 Bake tostadas until cheese melts; serve topped with fresh coriander leaves, if desired.

preparation time 10 minutes
cooking time 10 minutes
makes 24
per tostada 3.4g fat; 259kJ (62 cal)

BEAN & TOMATO TOSTADA WEDGES

Empanadas

An empanada is a small stuffed bread or pastry, Normally semi-circular in shape, they are stuffed with spiced meat, cheese or vegetables and deep fried or baked. Some Tex Mex restaurants even serve a sweet version – filled with caramelised apples.

EMPANADAS

BEAN NACHOS

420g can mexican-style beans, drained
300g can red kidney beans, rinsed, drained
and mashed
2 tablespoons tomato paste
1 tablespoon water
230g packet plain corn chips
1½ cups (185g) coarsely grated cheddar
cheese
1 large avocado (320g)
1 small red onion (100g), chopped finely
1 large tomato (250g), chopped finely
1 teaspoon lemon juice
½ cup (120g) soured cream
1 tablespoon coarsely chopped fresh
coriander

1 Preheat oven to moderately hot
(200°C/180°C fan-assisted). Heat combined
beans, paste and the water, stirring, in large
non-stick frying pan. Cover; keep warm.
2 Place corn chips in large ovenproof dish;
sprinkle with cheese. Bake about 5 minutes
or until cheese melts.
3 Meanwhile, mash avocado in small bowl;
stir in half of the combined onion and
tomato, and juice.
4 Top heated corn chips with bean mixture,
avocado mixture and sour cream; sprinkle
nachos with remaining onion and tomato,
and coriander.

preparation time 15 minutes
cooking time 10 minutes
serves 4
per serving 60g fat; 3840kJ (917 cal)

CHICKPEA CORN WRAPS

1 tablespoon olive oil
1 small onion (80g), chopped coarsely
1 clove garlic, crushed
1 teaspoon sweet paprika
½ teaspoon ground chilli powder
1 teaspoon ground cumin
400g can tomato puree
300g can chickpeas, rinsed, drained
1 tablespoon chopped fresh coriander
8 corn tortillas
1 small red onion (100g), chopped coarsely
1 medium tomato (190g), chopped coarsely
1 small avocado (200g), chopped coarsely
½ cup (60g) coarsely grated cheddar cheese
½ cup finely shredded iceberg lettuce

1 Heat oil in medium saucepan; cook onion
and garlic, stirring, until onion softens. Add
spices; cook, stirring, 2 minutes. Add puree;
bring to a boil. Reduce heat; simmer, stirring
occasionally, 5 minutes. Add chickpeas and
coriander; cook, stirring, until hot.
2 Soften tortillas in microwave oven on
HIGH (100%) for 30 seconds. Divide chickpea
mixture and remaining ingredients among
tortillas; fold enchiladas to enclose filling.

preparation time 15 minutes
cooking time 10 minutes
serves 4
per serving 21.2g fat; 1972kJ (472 cal)
tips We used 16cm-round corn tortillas,
which are vacuum-packed. Any unused
tortillas can be frozen in freezer bags for up
to 3 weeks. You can also soften tortillas by
wrapping them in foil and heating them in a
moderate oven about 5 minutes or until hot.

It's all about tortillas...

CHICKEN & AVOCADO TORTILLA WRAPS

1 large tomato (500g), chopped coarsely
1 medium avocado (500g), chopped coarsely
1 small red onion (100g), chopped coarsely
2 tablespoons coarsely chopped fresh
coriander
4 cups (400g) shredded cooked chicken
8 large flour tortillas

tomato salsa
2 medium tomatoes (300g), chopped finely
2 tablespoons pickled jalapeño chillies
¼ cup finely chopped fresh coriander
1 clove garlic, crushed
1 tablespoon lime juice

1 Make tomato salsa.
2 Combine tomato, avocado, onion,
coriander, ½ cup (130g) of the salsa and
chicken in large bowl.
3 Warm tortillas according to manufacturer's
instructions. Top each tortilla with about an
eighth of chicken filling; roll to enclose filling.
Repeat with remaining tortillas and chicken
filling. Serve with remaining salsa.

tomato salsa Combine ingredients in
medium bowl.

preparation time 15 minutes
cooking time 5 minutes
serves 4
per serving 34.2g fat; 2922kJ (699 cal)

PORK & CORN TORTILLA WRAPS

2 tablespoons vegetable oil
½ teaspoon dried oregano
1 teaspoon ground cumin
½ teaspoon chilli powder
600g pork fillet, sliced thinly
16 corn tortillas
310g can corn kernels, drained
3 medium tomatoes (450g), chopped
coarsely
1 small red onion (100g), chopped finely
½ cup coarsely chopped fresh coriander
1 round lettuce, torn
½ cup (120g) soured cream

1 Combine oil, oregano and spices in
medium bowl, add pork; toss pork to coat in
mixture. Cook pork in heated large non-stick
frying pan until cooked as desired.
2 Meanwhile, warm tortillas according to
manufacturer's instructions.
3 Combine corn, tomato, onion and
coriander in medium bowl.
4 Divide pork, salsa and remaining
ingredients among tortillas; roll to enclose
the filling.

preparation time 15 minutes
cooking time 15 minutes
serves 4
per serving 29.9g fat; 3574kJ (855 cal)

PORK & CORN WRAPS

CHICKEN & AVOCADO WRAPS

Tortillas

You don't have to look far to find a tortilla in Tex-Mex cuisine – they crop up everywhere. This versatile flatbread, made from corn or wheat, has been around for centuries. It can be deep fried to make crisp taco shells and chips, rolled and stuffed with a filling, dipped in a sauce – the possibilities are almost endless...

STEAK FAJITAS

3 cloves garlic, crushed
¼ cup (60ml) lemon juice
2 teaspoons ground cumin
1 tablespoon olive oil
600g grilling steak, cut into strips
1 large red pepper (350g), sliced thickly
1 large green pepper (350g), sliced thickly
1 medium yellow pepper (250g), sliced
thickly
1 large red onion (300g), sliced thickly
8 large flour tortillas

salsa cruda
2 medium tomatoes (300g), deseeded,
chopped finely
1 fresh long red chilli, chopped finely
½ cup coarsely chopped fresh coriander
1 clove garlic, crushed
1 small white onion (80g), chopped finely
2 tablespoons lime juice

1 Combine garlic, juice, cumin and oil in
large bowl; add beef, stir to coat in mixture.
Cover; refrigerate until required.
2 Make salsa cruda.
3 Cook beef, in batches, in oiled heated large
frying pan, stirring, until browned all over
and cooked as desired. Cover to keep warm.
Cook peppers and onion, in batches, in same
pan, stirring, until softened.
4 Meanwhile, heat tortillas.
5 Return beef and pepper mixture to pan;
stir gently over medium heat until hot. Divide
fajita mixture among serving plates; serve
with tortillas and salsa cruda and, if desired,
guacamole (see page 46).

salsa cruda Combine ingredients in a bowl.

preparation time 30 minutes

cooking time 15 minutes
serves 4
per serving 20.5g fat; 2646kJ (633 cal)

PORK CHIMICHANGAS

500g diced pork
2 black peppercorns
3 cloves garlic, peeled
3 cups (750ml) water
1 teaspoon salt
1 teaspoon ground cumin
½ cup chopped fresh coriander
1 small red onion (80g), chopped finely
2 fresh green jalapeño chillies, deseeded,
chopped finely
8 large flour tortillas
vegetable oil, for deep-frying

1 Combine pork, peppercorns, garlic, the
water, salt and cumin in large saucepan;
simmer, covered, about 1 hour or until pork
is tender; cool in liquid.
2 Drain liquid from pork, discard liquid and
peppercorns. Shred pork and garlic, using
two forks. Combine pork mixture, coriander,
onion and chilli in large bowl.
3 Divide pork mixture evenly between
tortillas. Roll tortillas up firmly, secure with
toothpick at each end of roll.
4 Heat oil in wok or large frying pan; deep-
fry rolls, in batches, until browned lightly.
Drain on kitchen paper.
5 Cut each chimichanga in half on an angle;
serve with guacamole (see page 46).

preparation time 40 minutes
cooking time 1 hour 10 minutes
(plus cooling time)
serves 8
per serving 14.8g fat; 1279kJ (306 cal)

STEAK FAJITAS

Chimichangas

A flour tortilla stuffed with a wide range of fillings, most commonly beans, rice, cheese, minced or shredded beef or chicken and rolled or folded into a package and deep-fried. They are often served with salsa, guacamole, soured cream or cheese.

PORK CHIMICHANGAS

CHICKEN QUESADILLAS

Quesadillas

A quesadilla is a Mexican snack food made from tortillas filled with cheese and vegetables or shredded or minced meat, which are then cooked until the cheese melts. They are usually served with fresh salsa.

SPINACH & CHEESE QUESADILLAS

SPINACH & CHEESE QUESADILLAS

⅔ cup (130g) low-fat cottage cheese
100g spinach leaves, trimmed
1 medium avocado (250g), chopped finely
1 cup (200g) canned mexican-style beans, drained
125g can corn kernels, drained
2 medium tomatoes (380g), deseeded, chopped finely
1 small red onion (100g), chopped finely
2 medium courgettes (240g), grated coarsely
16 small flour tortillas
1½ cups (150g) coarsely grated low-fat mozzarella cheese

1 Blend or process cottage cheese and spinach until smooth. Combine avocado, beans, corn, tomato, onion and courgette in medium bowl.
2 Place eight tortillas on lightly oiled oven tray; divide spinach mixture among tortillas, leaving 2cm border around edge. Divide avocado mixture among tortillas, sprinkling it over spinach mixture. Top each with one of the remaining tortillas.
3 Sprinkle mozzarella over quesadilla stacks; place under preheated grill until cheese just melts and browns lightly.

preparation time 20 minutes
cooking time 10 minutes
serves 8
per serving 11.8g fat; 1177kJ (282 cal)

CHICKEN QUESADILLAS

1 tablespoon olive oil
2 cloves garlic, crushed
1 small red onion (100g), chopped finely
¼ teaspoon cayenne pepper
2 teaspoons ground cumin
1 medium red pepper (200g), chopped finely
1 medium green pepper (200g), chopped finely
3 cups (480g) shredded cooked chicken
8 large flour tortillas
2 cups (240g) coarsely grated cheddar cheese

1 Heat oil in large frying pan; cook garlic and onion, stirring, until onion softens. Add spices and peppers; cook, stirring, until peppers soften. Remove from heat; stir in chicken.
2 Place one tortilla on board; top with ¼ cup of cheese, then quarter of chicken mixture, then another ¼ cup of cheese. Top with second tortilla. Repeat with remaining tortillas, cheese and chicken mixture.
3 Cook quesadillas, one at a time, uncovered, in same lightly oiled large frying pan, over medium heat, until golden brown. Turn quesadilla, browned-side up, onto large plate then carefully slide back into pan, uncooked-side down. Remove from pan when golden brown both sides; cover to keep warm while cooking remaining quesadillas.
4 Serve quesadillas, cut into quarters, with guacamole (see page 46), dollop of soured cream and shredded lettuce, if desired.

preparation time 15 minutes
cooking time 30 minutes
serves 4
per serving 40.7g fat; 3352kJ (802 cal)

Enchiladas

An enchilada is a corn tortilla rolled around a filling, covered with a sauce and then baked. They can be filled with a variety of ingredients, including meat, chicken, beans, cheese, vegetables, seafood or a combinations of fillings.

CHICKEN ENCHILADAS

3 chipotle chillies
1 cup (250ml) boiling water
500g chicken breast fillets
1 tablespoon vegetable oil
1 large red onion (300g), chopped finely
2 cloves garlic, crushed
1 teaspoon ground cumin
1 tablespoon tomato paste
2 x 425g cans crushed tomatoes
1 tablespoon finely chopped fresh oregano
⅔ cup (160g) soured cream
1½ cups (240g) coarsely grated cheddar cheese
10 small flour tortillas

1 Cover chillies with the water in small heatproof bowl; stand 20 minutes. Remove stems from chillies; discard stems. Blend or process chillies with soaking liquid until smooth.
2 Meanwhile, place chicken in medium saucepan of boiling water. Return to a boil then reduce heat; simmer, covered, about 10 minutes or until chicken is cooked through. Remove chicken from poaching liquid; cool 10 minutes. Discard poaching liquid; shred chicken finely.
3 Preheat oven to moderate (180°C/160°C fan-assisted). Lightly oil shallow rectangular 3-litre (12-cup) ovenproof dish.
4 Heat oil in large frying pan; cook onion, stirring, until softened. Reserve half of onion in small bowl.
5 Add garlic and cumin to remaining onion in pan; cook, stirring, until fragrant. Add chilli mixture, tomato paste, undrained tomatoes and oregano. Bring to a boil then reduce heat; simmer, uncovered, 1 minute. Remove sauce from heat.

6 Meanwhile, combine shredded chicken, reserved onion, half of soured cream and third of cheese in medium bowl.
7 Heat tortillas according to manufacturer's instructions. Dip tortillas, one at a time, in tomato sauce in pan; place on board. Place ¼ cup of chicken mixture along edge of each tortilla; roll enchiladas to enclose filling.
8 Spread ½ cup tomato sauce into prepared dish. Place enchiladas, seam-side down, in dish (they should fit snugly, without overcrowding). Pour remaining tomato sauce over enchiladas; sprinkle with remaining cheese. Cook, uncovered, about 15 minutes or until cheese melts and enchiladas are heated through. Sprinkle with coriander leaves, if desired. Serve with remaining soured cream.

preparation time 50 minutes
(plus standing time)
cooking time 35 minutes
serves 10
per serving 9.4g fat; 1593kJ (381 cal)

BEEF & BEAN TACOS

2 cloves garlic, crushed
400g minced beef
1 teaspoon chilli powder
1 teaspoon ground cumin
2 x 300g cans red kidney beans, rinsed,
drained
⅓ cup tomato paste
1 cup (250ml) water
2 medium tomatoes (380g), chopped
8 taco shells
½ small iceberg lettuce, shredded finely

salsa cruda
½ cucumber (130g), deseeded, chopped
finely
1 small red onion (80g), chopped finely
2 small tomatoes (260g), deseeded, chopped
2 teaspoons mild chilli sauce

1 Preheat oven to180°C (160°C fan-assisted).
2 Heat lightly oiled large non-stick frying
pan; cook garlic and beef, stirring, until beef
is browned all over. Add chilli, cumin, beans,
paste, the water and tomato; cook, covered,
over low heat about 15 minutes or until
mixture thickens slightly.
3 Meanwhile, heat taco shells, upside down,
uncovered, on oven tray in oven for
5 minutes.
4 Just before serving, fill shells with beef
mixture, lettuce and salsa cruda.

salsa cruda Combine ingredients together
in small bowl.

preparation time 15 minutes
cooking time 20 minutes
serves 4
per serving 4.9g fat; 723kJ (173 cal)

BEEF BURRITOS

1 tablespoon olive oil
500g minced beef
1 medium onion (150g), chopped finely
1 clove garlic, crushed
1 teaspoon ground cumin
¼ teaspoon chilli powder
400g can crushed tomatoes
½ cup (125ml) water
300g can red kidney beans, rinsed, drained
4 large flour tortillas
1 cup (125g) coarsely grated cheddar
1 teaspoon hot paprika
¾ cup (180g) soured cream
1 tablespoon chopped fresh coriander

1 Heat oil in medium frying pan; cook beef,
stirring, until browned. Add onion, garlic and
spices; cook, stirring, until onion softens.
Stir in undrained crushed tomatoes, the
water and beans; simmer, uncovered, about
15 minutes or until mixture thickens.
2 Preheat oven to 200°C (180°C fan-assisted).
3 Divide warm beef filling among tortillas,
roll; secure with toothpicks.
4 Place filled tortillas on oiled oven tray;
sprinkle with cheese and paprika. Bake about
10 minutes or until heated through. Remove
toothpicks; serve topped with sour cream,
coriander and, if desired, guacamole (see
page 46).

preparation time 20 minutes
cooking time 35 minutes
serves 4
per serving 45.4g fat; 3110kJ (744 cal)

BEEF BURRITOS

Tacos & Burritos

Tacos are crisp-fried corn tortillas filled with spiced ground beef or chicken, cheese, lettuce, tomato or soured cream. A burrito is a flour tortilla wrapped or folded around a filling of beans, lettuce, salsa, meat, avocado, cheese, spicy rice and soured cream.

BEEF & BEAN TACOS

Classic chilli

CHILLI CON CARNE WITH CORN DUMPLINGS

2 tablespoons olive oil
1.5kg braising steak, diced into 4cm pieces
2 medium onions (300g), chopped
2 cloves garlic, crushed
1 large green pepper (350g), chopped
2 teaspoons sweet paprika
2 teaspoons ground cumin
2 teaspoons chilli powder
800g can whole peeled tomatoes
2 tablespoons tomato paste
1 cup (250ml) beef stock
400g can red kidney beans, rinsed, drained

corn dumplings
½ cup (75g) self-raising flour
½ cup (85g) polenta
50g butter, chopped
1 egg, beaten lightly
¼ cup (30g) coarsely grated cheddar cheese
¼ cup coarsely chopped fresh coriander
130g can corn kernels, drained
1 tablespoon milk, approximately

1 Heat half the oil in large saucepan; cook steak, in batches, until browned.
2 Heat remaining oil in same pan; cook onion, garlic and pepper, stirring, until vegetables soften. Add spices; cook, stirring until fragrant.
3 Return steak to pan with undrained tomatoes, paste and stock; bring to the boil. Reduce heat; simmer, covered, for 2½ hours or until tender.

4 Shred a quarter of the steak coarsely with two forks, add meat to pan with kidney beans; bring to the boil. Simmer, uncovered, for 15 minutes.
5 Meanwhile, make corn dumplings. Drop level tablespoons of dumpling mixture, about 2cm apart, on top of steak mixture. Simmer, covered, about 20 minutes or until dumplings are cooked through.

corn dumplings Place flour and polenta in a medium bowl; rub in butter. Stir in egg, cheese, coriander, corn and enough milk for a soft, sticky dough.

preparation time 25 minutes
cooking time 3 hours 30 minutes
serves 6
per serving 28.2g fat; 2784kJ (666 cal)

Sticky ribs

TEXAN-STYLE SPARE RIBS

3kg american-style pork spare ribs
2 tablespoons sweet paprika
1 tablespoon ground cumin
1 teaspoon cayenne pepper
2 x 800ml bottles beer
1 cup (250ml) barbecue sauce
¼ cup (60ml) water
¼ cup (60ml) maple syrup
¼ cup (60ml) cider vinegar

TEX-MEX RIBS

1 Place ribs on large tray. Combine spices in small bowl, rub spice mixture all over ribs. Cover; refrigerate 3 hours or overnight.
2 Preheat oven to moderate (180°C/160°C fan-assisted).
3 Bring beer to a boil in medium saucepan. Reduce heat; simmer, uncovered, 20 minutes. Divide beer and ribs between two large shallow baking dishes; cook, covered, 1½ hours. Remove from oven; discard beer.
4 Meanwhile, combine sauce, the water, syrup and vinegar in small saucepan; bring to a boil. Reduce heat; simmer, uncovered, 5 minutes.
5 Cook ribs, in batches, on heated barbecue (or grill or grill plate), turning and brushing with sauce occasionally, until browned all over.

preparation time 20 minutes
(plus refrigeration time)
cooking time 2 hours 5 minutes
serves 8
per serving 17.5g fat; 2123kJ (cal 508)

TEX-MEX RIBS

1 cup (250ml) barbecue sauce
2 teaspoons chilli powder
2 x 35g packets taco seasoning
2kg american-style pork spare ribs

1 Combine sauce, chilli powder and seasoning in large shallow dish; add ribs. Cover; refrigerate 3 hours or overnight.
2 Cook ribs, in batches, on heated barbecue (or grill or grill plate), or roast in a moderate oven, about 45 minutes or until ribs are cooked through, turning and brushing with sauce during cooking, until browned all over and cooked through.

preparation time 5 minutes
(plus marinating time)
cooking time 45 minutes
serves 4
per serving 31.2g fat; 2455kJ (586 cal)

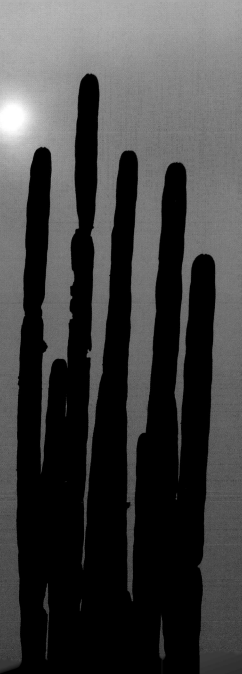

CHILLI-BEEF RIBS

2 cups (500ml) tomato sauce
½ cup (125ml) worcestershire sauce
¾ cup (180ml) vegetable oil
½ cup (125ml) water
¼ cup (60ml) white vinegar
⅓ cup (75g) firmly packed brown sugar
1 medium onion (150g), chopped finely
1 long green chilli, deseeded, chopped finely
1.5kg beef spare ribs

1 Combine sauces, oil, the water, vinegar,
sugar, onion and chilli in large dish; add ribs.
Cover; refrigerate 3 hours or overnight.
2 Drain ribs; reserve marinade.
3 Place reserved marinade in small saucepan;
bring to a boil. Reduce heat; simmer, uncovered,
until thickened slightly.
4 Cook ribs on heated oiled barbecue,
uncovered, until browned and cooked through.
Pour sauce over ribs and serve.

preparation time 10 minutes
(plus marinating time)
cooking time 20 minutes
serves 4
per serving 54.1g fat; 3999kJ (955 cal)
tip The ribs can also be roasted in a moderate
oven ubtil browned and cooked through.

Rice & beans

BLACK BEAN & CHIPOTLE STEW

1½ cups (300g) dried black beans
2 chipotle chillies
½ cup (125ml) boiling water
1 tablespoon cumin seeds
2 trimmed corn cobs (500g)
2 teaspoons olive oil
1 large onion (200g), chopped finely
810g can crushed tomatoes
8 white corn tortillas

classic salsa
1 small red onion (100g), chopped coarsely
1 small tomato (90g), chopped coarsely
½ cup coarsely chopped fresh coriander
½ cucumber (130g), chopped coarsely
1 tablespoon olive oil
2 tablespoons lemon juice

1 Place beans in bowl, cover with water; stand overnight, drain. Rinse under cold water; drain. Place beans in saucepan of boiling water. Return to a boil then reduce heat; simmer, uncovered, about 15 minutes or until beans are just tender. Drain.
2 Preheat oven to moderately hot (200°C/180°C fan-assisted).
3 Place chillies and the boiling water in bowl; stand 15 minutes. Discard stalks; blend or process chilli and soaking liquid until smooth.
4 Meanwhile, dry-fry cumin seeds in small frying pan, stirring, until fragrant.
5 Cook corn under heated grill until browned lightly and just tender. When cooled, cut kernels from cobs with sharp knife.
6 Heat oil in large flameproof dish; cook onion, stirring, until soft. Add drained beans, chilli mixture, cumin, undrained tomatoes and half of corn; bring to a boil. Cook in oven about 20 minutes or until sauce thickens.
7 Combine remaining corn with salsa ingredients in medium bowl. Meanwhile, heat tortillas. Serve stew with tortillas and salsa.

preparation time 15 minutes (plus standing time)
cooking time 1 hour
serves 4
per serving 10.4g fat; 1839kJ (440 cal)

SPICY CORN & BEAN STEW

2 teaspoons olive oil
1 medium green pepper (200g), sliced thinly
1 medium onion (150g), sliced thinly
1 cup (165g) fresh corn kernels
3 tomatoes (450g), chopped coarsely
420g can kidney beans, rinsed, drained
1 fresh long green chilli, chopped finely
8 corn tortillas, warmed

1 Heat half the oil in large pan; cook pepper, stirring, until just tender. Remove from pan.
2 Heat remaining oil in same pan; cook onion and corn, stirring, until onion softens. Add tomato, beans and chilli; simmer, uncovered, 10 minutes.
3 Stir pepper into tomato mixture; serve with warm tortillas.

preparation time 15 minutes
cooking time 15 minutes
serves 4
per serving 9.9g fat; 1935kJ (463 cal)

BLACK BEAN & CHIPOLTE STEW

SPICY CORN & BEAN STEW

BARBECUED CORN WITH CHUNKY SALSA & RICE

4 untrimmed corn cobs (1.6kg)
2 teaspoons groundnut oil
2 cloves garlic, crushed
1 small white onion (80g), chopped finely
1 small red pepper (150g), chopped finely
1 fresh long red chilli, chopped finely
1½ cups (300g) white medium-grain rice
1 cup (250ml) vegetable stock
1 cup (250ml) water

chunky salsa
3 tomatoes (450g), chopped coarsely
1 small white onion (80g), chopped finely
¼ cup (60g) pickled jalapeño chillies
½ cup coarsely chopped fresh coriander
1 clove garlic, crushed
2 tablespoons lime juice

1 Gently peel husk down corn cob, keeping husk attached at base. Remove as much silk as possible then bring husk back over cob to re-wrap and enclose completely. Place corn in large bowl, add enough cold water to completely submerge corn.
2 Heat oil in medium saucepan; cook garlic, onion, pepper and chilli, stirring, until onion softens. Add rice; cook, stirring, 1 minute. Add stock and the water. Bring to a boil then reduce heat; simmer, covered, about 20 minutes or until rice is just tender. Remove from heat; fluff rice with fork.
3 Meanwhile, drain corn. Cook corn on heated oiled grill plate (or grill or barbecue) about 25 minutes or until corn is tender, turning occasionally.
4 Make chunky salsa.
5 Serve corn with rice and salsa.

chunky salsa Combine ingredients for chunky salsa in medium bowl.

preparation time 20 minutes
(plus refrigeration time)
cooking time 30 minutes
serves 4
per serving 6.7g fat; 2541kJ (608 cal)

DRUNKEN BEANS

1 cup (200g) dried pinto beans
3 bacon rashers (210g), rind removed, chopped coarsely
1 medium onion (150g), chopped finely
1 clove garlic, crushed
1 teaspoon ground cumin
½ teaspoon cayenne pepper
1 tablespoon tomato paste
425g can crushed tomatoes
1 cup (250ml) water
1 cup (250ml) beer
1 tablespoon worcestershire sauce
2 tablespoons brown sugar

1 Place beans in medium bowl, cover with water; stand overnight. Drain.
2 Cook bacon, onion, garlic and spices in lightly oiled large saucepan, stirring, until onion softens. Add drained beans and remaining ingredients. Bring to a boil then reduce heat; simmer, covered, about 1½ hours or until beans are just tender.

preparation time 10 minutes
(plus standing time)
cooking time 1 hour 40 minutes
serves 4
per serving 5.1g fat; 1196kJ (286 cal)

PINEAPPLE & MINT MARGARITA

Salting glass rims

Rub the flesh of a lime or lemon around the rim of your chosen glass until the whole rim has been evenly moistened with juice. Turn the glass upside down and dip the rim into a saucer filled with coarse-grained salt. Shake away any excess.

FROZEN TEQUILA SUNRISE

Sundowners ... and risers

MARGARITA

45ml tequila
30ml fresh lime juice
30ml Cointreau
1 cup ice cubes

1 Combine ingredients in a cocktail shaker.
2 Shake vigorously then strain into a
salt-rimmed 150ml margarita glass.
3 Garnish with a slice of lemon.

makes 1
tips You can use triple sec or white curaçao
instead of Cointreau, if you prefer.

PINEAPPLE & MINT MARGARITA

30ml tequila
15ml Cointreau
30ml fresh lime juice
30ml bottled pineapple juice
4 fresh mint leaves
1 cup ice cubes

1 Combine ingredients in jug of a blender;
blend on high speed until well combined.
2 Pour mixture into a salt-rimmed 150ml
cocktail glass.
3 Garnish with a small wedge of lemon and
a sprig of mint.

makes 1

TEQUILA SUNRISE

30ml tequila
120ml orange juice
7ml grenadine
ice

1 Pour tequila and orange juice, one after the
other, over ice in 285ml highball glass.
2 Drop grenadine through centre of cocktail.
3 Garnish with a orange slice and a red
cherry.

makes 1

FROZEN TEQUILA SUNRISE

30ml tequila
90ml orange juice
concentrate, frozen
1½ cups ice cubes
10ml grenadine

1 Combine tequila, juice and ice in jug
of a blender; blend until smooth, pour
into 300ml highball glass.
2 Carefully drizzle grenadine, over the
back of a tablespoon, around inside rim
of glass.
3 Garnish with a straw.

makes 1

A taste of the Deep South

Southern-style cooking is a rich, spicy cuisine based around locally-sourced ingredients. It is a fusion of many different cultural influences, including those of many refugees and colonists to the area, such as the French-speaking Cajuns expelled from Canada, the Creole settlers of colonial French Louisiana and West Africans, all brought to the region their own ingredients and different styles of cooking, which are now blended together and often referred to as 'soul food'.

Soups & stews

CHICKEN, CHORIZO & OKRA GUMBO

1.5kg chicken
1 medium onion (150g), chopped coarsely
2 medium carrots (240g), chopped coarsely
2 celery sticks (150g), chopped coarsely
1 bay leaf
12 black peppercorns
3 litres water (12 cups)
60g butter
2 cloves garlic, crushed
1 small onion (80g), chopped finely
1 medium red pepper (200g), chopped finely
1 teaspoon sweet paprika
¼ teaspoon ground cayenne
¼ teaspoon ground cloves
2 teaspoons dried oregano
¼ cup plain flour (35g)
¼ cup tomato paste (60g)
2 tablespoons worcestershire sauce
400g can tomatoes
200g fresh okra
1 cup short grain rice (200g)
200g chorizo sausage, sliced thinly

1 Rinse chicken under cold water, pat dry with absorbent paper.
2 Combine chicken, medium onion, carrot, celery, bay leaf, peppercorns and the water in large saucepan; bring to a boil. Simmer, covered, 1½ hours, skimming occasionally; strain through muslin-lined strainer into large bowl. Reserve stock and chicken; discard vegetables.
3 When chicken is cool enough to handle, remove and discard skin. Remove meat from carcass; shred meat, discard bones.

> Gumbo is a hearty stew that originated in Louisiana. The one essential to all versions is the inclusion of okra – the word gumbo is actually the word for okra in some West African dialects, and the recipe was introduced to the Deep South by African slaves. The okra acts as a thickening agent, as does the roux, and is what makes it a stew rather than a soup.

4 Melt butter in large saucepan; cook garlic and small onion, stirring, until onion is soft. Add pepper, paprika, cayenne, clove and oregano; cook, stirring, about 2 minutes or until fragrant.
5 Stir in flour; cook, stirring, until mixture thickens and bubbles. Gradually stir in reserved stock, paste, sauce and undrained crushed tomatoes; stir until mixture boils and thickens. Stir in halved okra and rice; simmer, uncovered, stirring occasionally, about 15 minutes or until both okra and rice are tender.
6 Meanwhile, heat large non-stick frying pan; cook sausage, in batches, until browned, drain on absorbent paper.
7 Add reserved chicken and sausage; stir gumbo over heat until heated through.

preparation time 30 minutes
cooking time 2 hours 15 minutes
serves 6
per serving 22.2g fat; 2116kJ (505 cal)

BLACK-EYED BEAN, OKRA & SWEET POTATO GUMBO

1 cup (200g) black-eyed beans
2 teaspoons olive oil
1 large onion (200g), chopped coarsely
3 cloves garlic, crushed
1 teaspoon dried thyme
2 teaspoons dried oregano
3 teaspoons ground fennel
1 teaspoon cayenne pepper
500g okra
600g sweet potatoes, chopped coarsely
2 x 425g cans crushed tomatoes
1 cup (250ml) water
1½ cups (300g) white long-grain rice
425g can baby corn, rinsed, drained

1 Place beans in medium bowl; cover with water, stand overnight, drain. Rinse under cold water; drain. Place beans in medium saucepan of boiling water; return to the boil. Reduce heat; simmer, uncovered, about 30 minutes or until beans are just tender.
2 Heat oil in large pan; cook onion and garlic, stirring, until onion softens. Add dried herbs and spices; cook, stirring, until fragrant.
3 Add drained beans, okra, sweet potato, undrained tomatoes and the water; bring to the boil. Reduce heat; simmer, uncovered, about 30 minutes until vegetables are tender.
4 Meanwhile, cook rice in pan of boiling water, uncovered, until just tender; drain.
5 Stir corn into gumbo; cook, uncovered, until corn is heated through. Serve gumbo with rice.

preparation time 15 minutes
(plus standing time)
cooking time 1 hour 15 minutes
serves 6
per serving 3.9g fat; 1881kJ (450 cal)

BLACK-EYED BEAN, BEEF & SPINACH SOUP

1 cup (200g) black-eyed beans
1 tablespoon olive oil
1 medium onion (150g), chopped finely
1 clove garlic, crushed
2.5 litres beef stock (10 cups)
¼ cup (60ml) dry red wine
2 tablespoons tomato paste
500g piece beef rump steak
250g trimmed spinach, chopped coarsely

1 Place beans in medium bowl, cover with water; stand overnight, drain. Rinse under cold water; drain.
2 Heat oil in large saucepan; cook onion and garlic, stirring, until onion softens. Add stock, wine, paste and beef to pan; bring to the boil. Reduce heat; simmer, covered, 40 minutes. Uncover; simmer 30 minutes.
3 Remove beef from pan. Add beans to pan; bring to the boil. Reduce heat; simmer, uncovered, until beans are tender.
4 Meanwhile, when beef is cool enough to handle, remove and discard fat and sinew. Chop beef coarsely; return to pan with spinach; simmer, uncovered, until soup is hot.

preparation time 5 minutes
(plus standing time)
cooking time 1 hour 50 minutes
serves 4
per serving 13.9g fat; 2199kJ (526 cal)
tip You need 1kg of untrimmed spinach to get the amount of trimmed spinach required for this recipe.

BLACK-EYED BEAN, OKRA & SWEET POTATO GUMBO

In the South, it's thought to be lucky to eat black-eyed beans on New Year's Day. This dates back to the time of the American Civil War when Union troops were ordered to strip the countryside of all food, crops, and livestock. At the time, Northerners considered black-eyed beans as animal fodder, and so they left this humble but nourishing food alone.

BLACK-EYED BEAN, BEEF & SPINACH SOUP

Corn bread

CORN BREAD

2 teaspoons (7g) dried yeast
125ml warm water
125ml warm milk
300g plain flour
85g polenta
½ teaspoon salt
2 teaspoons polenta, extra

1 Mix yeast with the water in small bowl; stir in milk. Sift flour into large bowl; stir in polenta and salt. Stir in yeast mixture; mix to a firm dough. Knead dough on floured surface about 10 minutes or until dough is smooth and elastic; place dough in greased large bowl. Cover; stand in warm place about 1 hour or until doubled in size.
2 Turn dough onto floured surface; knead further 5 minutes. Shape dough into 13cm round; place on lightly greased oven tray. Using sharp knife, cut 1cm deep cross into top of dough. Stand, covered, in warm place 20 minutes; sprinkle with extra polenta.
3 Bake, uncovered, in moderately hot oven for about 20 minutes or until bread sounds hollow when tapped.

preparation time 25 minutes
(plus standing time)
cooking time 20 minutes
makes 1 loaf
per loaf 10.7g fat; 1017kJ (243 cal)

CHILLI CORN BREAD

1 cup (150g) self-raising flour
1 teaspoon salt
1 cup (170g) polenta
½ cup (100g) kibbled rye
1 tablespoon brown sugar
1 teaspoon ground cumin
½ cup (60g) finely grated cheddar cheese
2 tablespoons finely chopped fresh flat-leaf parsley
1 teaspoon finely chopped fresh thyme
310g can creamed corn
⅔ cup (90g) frozen corn kernels, thawed
⅔ cup (160ml) buttermilk
⅓ cup (80ml) milk
2 teaspoons finely chopped fresh chilli
2 eggs
50g butter, melted

1 Preheat oven to 200°C/180°C fan-assisted. Oil deep 19cm-square cake tin; line base with baking parchment.
2 Sift flour and salt into large bowl; stir in polenta. Combine remaining ingredients in medium bowl; stir into dry ingredients. Spread mixture into tin.
3 Bake bread about 1 hour. Stand 10 minutes; turn onto wire rack to cool.

preparation time 20 minutes
cooking time 1 hour (plus cooling time)
serves 10
per slice 3.6g fat; 426kj (102 cal)
tip You can use well-drained canned corn kernels (or fresh/cooked) instead of the frozen corn if you like.

CORN BREAD

Corn bread is a popular staple food enjoyed all over the southern states for its texture and aroma. It can be baked, fried or even steamed, although steamed corn bread is mushy and more like a pudding than traditional corn bread.

CHILLI CORN BREAD

HONEY MUSTARD GLAZED RIBS

STICKY RIBS

Finger-lickin' ribs

HONEY MUSTARD GLAZED RIBS

½ cup (125ml) orange juice
½ cup (175g) honey
½ cup (125ml) barbecue sauce
2 tablespoons soy sauce
1 tablespoon wholegrain mustard
3 cloves garlic, crushed
2kg american-style pork spare ribs

1 Combine juice, honey, sauces, mustard and garlic in large shallow dish; add pork. Cover; refrigerate 3 hours or overnight.
2 Drain pork; reserve marinade.
3 Place ribs in disposable baking dish. Cook ribs in covered barbecue, using indirect heat, following manufacturer's instructions, about 45 minutes or until cooked through, brushing ribs occasionally with reserved marinade during cooking. Sprinkle with orange rind and coriander, if desired.

preparation time 10 minutes
(plus marinating time)
cooking time 45 minutes
serves 4
per serving 30.4g fat; 2705kJ (646 cal)

STICKY PORK RIBS

2 tablespoons tomato paste
2 tablespoons tomato sauce
2 tablespoons soy sauce
1 teaspoon grated lemon rind
¼ cup (60ml) lemon juice
1 tablespoon brown sugar
1 teaspoon cracked black pepper
1 teaspoon ground allspice
¼ teaspoon chilli powder
2 cloves garlic, crushed
2kg american-style pork spare ribs

1 Combine paste, sauces, rind, juice, sugar, pepper, allspice, chilli powder and garlic in large shallow dish; add pork. Cover; refrigerate 3 hours or overnight.
2 Remove ribs from marinade; reserve marinade.
3 Place ribs in disposable baking dish. Cook ribs in covered barbecue, using indirect heat, following manufacturer's instructions, about 45 minutes or until ribs are cooked through, brushing ribs occasionally with reserved marinade during cooking.

preparation time 10 minutes
(plus marinating time)
cooking time 45 minutes
serves 4
per serving 30.4g fat; 1968kJ (470 cal)

Soul food

CHILLI PORK CUTLETS WITH PUMPKIN CHIPS

3 long green chillies, chopped coarsely
3 spring onions, chopped coarsely
2 cloves garlic, crushed
1 teaspoon ground allspice
1 teaspoon dried thyme
1 teaspoon white sugar
1 tablespoon light soy sauce
1 tablespoon lime juice
4 x 280g pork loin chops
1kg piece pumpkin, trimmed
2 tablespoons vegetable oil

chilli dipping sauce
⅓ cup (100g) mayonnaise
2 tablespoons chilli sauce

1 Combine chilli, onion, garlic, allspice, thyme, sugar, sauce, juice and pork in medium bowl.
2 Combine ingredients for chilli dipping sauce in small bowl.
3 Cut pumpkin into 7cm chips; boil, steam or microwave until tender. Drain; combine chips with oil in medium bowl. Cook chips on heated oiled grill plate until browned.
4 Meanwhile, cook pork on grill plate until cooked. Serve pork with chips and dipping sauce.

preparation time 15 minutes
cooking time 25 minutes
serves 4
per serving 39g fat; 2554kJ (611 cal)

CHILLI PORK CUTLETS

PORK & BLACK-EYED BEANS

PORK & BLACK-EYED BEANS

1 cup (200g) black-eyed beans
1kg pork neck, sliced thickly
⅓ cup (50g) plain flour
2 tablespoons olive oil
1 medium onion (150g), chopped coarsely
2 cloves garlic, crushed
½ teaspoon five-spice powder
1 teaspoon black peppercorns, crushed coarsely
½ teaspoon chilli powder
½ cup (125ml) dry white wine
3 cups (750ml) chicken stock
½ cup coarsely chopped fresh flat-leaf parsley

1 Place beans in medium bowl, cover with cold water; stand overnight, drain. Rinse under cold water; drain.

2 Coat pork in flour, shake away excess. Heat half the oil in large flameproof casserole dish; cook pork, in batches, until browned all over.
3 Heat remaining oil in same dish; cook onion, garlic, five-spice, pepper and chilli, stirring, until spices are fragrant and onion softens. Add beans, wine and stock; bring to a boil.
4 Return pork to dish; simmer, covered, 40 minutes. Uncover; simmer about 30 minutes or until pork is tender and sauce thickens slightly, stirring occasionally. Remove from heat; stir in rind and parsley.

preparation time 20 minutes
(plus standing time)
cooking time 1 hour 30 minutes
serves 4
per serving 19.9g fat; 2608kJ (624 cal)

Southern-style chicken

DEEP-SOUTH WINGS

16 small chicken wings (1.3kg)
¼ cup (60ml) tomato sauce
¼ cup (60ml) worcestershire sauce
¼ cup (55g) brown sugar
1 tablespoon american mustard

dipping sauce
1 tablespoon american mustard
2 tablespoons tomato sauce
1 tablespoon worcestershire sauce
2 tablespoons brown sugar

1 Preheat oven to 220°C/200°C fan-assisted.
2 Cut wings into three pieces at joints; discard tips. Combine chicken with remaining ingredients in large bowl. Cover; refrigerate 3 hours or overnight.
3 Place chicken, in single layer, on oiled wire rack set inside large shallow baking dish; brush remaining marinade over chicken. Roast about 30 minutes or until chicken is cooked through.
4 Make dipping sauce; serve with the chicken wings.

dipping sauce Combine ingredients in small bowl; cook, covered, in microwave oven on HIGH (100%) for 1 minute.

preparation time 10 minutes
(plus refrigeration time)
cooking time 30 minutes
makes 32
per wing 1.4g fat; 213kJ (51 cal)

CAJUN CHICKEN WITH PINEAPPLE SALSA

1 tablespoon sweet paprika
1 teaspoon cayenne pepper
2 teaspoons garlic powder
2 teaspoons dried oregano
1 tablespoon olive oil
8 chicken thigh fillets (880g)

pineapple salsa
4 bacon rashers (280g), rind removed
1 small pineapple (800g), chopped finely
1 small red thai chilli, chopped finely
¼ cup coarsely chopped flat-leaf parsley
1 medium red pepper (200g), chopped coarsely
¼ cup (60ml) lime juice
1 teaspoon olive oil

1 Combine spices, oregano and oil in large bowl; add chicken, toss to coat in mixture.
2 Make pineapple salsa.
3 Meanwhile, cook chicken on heated oiled flat plate, uncovered, until cooked through.
4 Serve chicken with pineapple salsa and lemon wedges, if desired.

pineapple salsa Grill bacon until crisp; drain, then chop coarsely. Place bacon in medium bowl with remaining ingredients; toss gently to combine.

preparation time 15 minutes
cooking time 15 minutes
serves 4
per serving 26.7g fat; 2011kJ (481 cal)

DEEP-SOUTH WINGS

Cajun cooking is a meeting of French and Southern American cuisines. A robust, country-style cooking , it makes generous use of spices – especially pepper and chilli. It originated from Acadian French-speaking refugees deported by the British from their lands in Canada to Louisiana in the 18th century.

CAJUN CHICKEN

SOUTHERN FRIED CHICKEN WITH BUTTERMILK MASH & GRAVY

20 chicken drumsticks (1.4kg)
1 cup (250ml) buttermilk
1 cup (150g) plain flour
¼ cup cajun seasoning
½ cup (125ml) vegetable oil
40g butter
5 medium potatoes (1kg), chopped coarsely
¾ cup (180ml) buttermilk, warmed, extra
40g butter, extra
250g green beans, trimmed, cut into
4cm lengths
2 cups (500ml) chicken stock

1 Combine chicken and buttermilk in large bowl. Cover; refrigerate 3 hours or overnight. Drain; discard buttermilk.
2 Combine flour and seasoning in large bowl; add chicken, toss to coat in mixture. Cover; refrigerate about 30 minutes or until flour forms a paste.
3 Preheat oven to 240°C/220°C fan-assisted.
4 Heat oil and butter in large deep frying pan; shake excess paste from chicken back into bowl. Cook chicken, in batches, over medium heat until browned and crisp.
5 Place chicken on oiled wire rack over large baking dish; roast, covered, in oven 15 minutes. Uncover; roast about 10 minutes or until chicken is cooked through and crisp.
6 Meanwhile, boil, steam or microwave potato until tender; drain. Mash with extra buttermilk and extra butter until smooth. Cover to keep warm.
7 Boil, steam or microwave beans until tender; drain.

8 To make gravy, add excess paste to pan; cook, stirring, until mixture bubbles. Gradually stir in stock; cook, stirring, until gravy boils and thickens. Strain gravy into large jug.
9 Serve chicken with mashed potato, beans and gravy.

preparation time 20 minutes
(plus refrigeration time)
cooking time 40 minutes
serves 4
per serving 69.7g fat; 4585kJ (1097 cal)
tip Cajun seasoning is available from the spice section at the supermarket.

JAMBALAYA

1 chorizo sausage (170g), sliced thickly
4 chicken drumsticks (600g)
4 chicken thighs (800g)
2 medium onions (300g), chopped finely
1½ cups (300g) white long-grain rice
¼ teaspoon cayenne pepper
2 teaspoons fresh thyme leaves
2 dried bay leaves
4 cloves garlic, crushed
3 trimmed celery stalks (300g), sliced thickly
3 cups (750ml) chicken stock
400g can crushed tomatoes
1 cup (120g) frozen peas

1 Cook chorizo in large saucepan, stirring, until browned all over; remove from pan.
2 Cook chicken, in batches, in same pan, until browned all over.
3 Cook onion in same pan, stirring, until onion softens. Add rice, cayenne, thyme, bay leaves, garlic, celery, stock, undrained tomatoes, chorizo and chicken; bring to a boil. Reduce heat; simmer, uncovered, about 15 minutes or until rice is tender and chicken is cooked through.
4 Add peas; cook, uncovered, about 5 minutes or until peas are tender.

preparation time 10 minutes
cooking time I hour
serves 4
per serving 44.9g fat; 3942kJ (943 cal)

SPEEDY CAJUN CHICKEN WITH TOMATO SALSA

750g chicken breast fillets, sliced thinly
¼ cup (18g) cajun seasoning
2 teaspoons grated lime rind
2 trimmed corn cobs (500g)
2 tablespoons olive oil
1 small red onion (100g), cut into thin wedges

tomato salsa
2 small plum tomatoes (120g), chopped finely
2 spring onions, sliced thinly
2 teaspoons lime juice
2 teaspoons balsamic vinegar

1 Combine chicken, seasoning and rind in large bowl; mix well. Cut kernels from corn.
2 Heat half of the oil in wok or large frying pan; stir-fry chicken mixture, in batches, until cooked through.
3 Heat remaining oil in wok; stir-fry corn and onion until onion is soft.
4 Return chicken to wok; stir-fry until hot.
5 Serve chicken topped with tomato salsa.

tomato salsa Combine ingredients in small bowl; mix well.

preparation time 20 minutes
cooking time 15 minutes
serves 4
per serving 21.2g fat; 1877kJ (449 cal)
tip Recipe best made just before serving; serve with soured cream, if desired.

JAMBALAYA

A creole version of paella, jambalaya is believed to have got its name when a cook in New Orleans named Jean tossed together ('balayez', in the Louisiana dialect) various leftovers that resulted in such a delicious dish that it was celebrated with a recipe called 'Jean balayez'.

SPEEDY CAJUN CHICKEN

Straight off the grill

CHILLI-RUBBED HICKORY-SMOKED RIB-EYE STEAKS

1 tablespoon finely grated lemon rind
2 teaspoons chilli powder
2 teaspoons dried thyme
1 teaspoon sweet smoked paprika
2 tablespoons olive oil
2 cloves garlic, crushed
4 x 200g beef rib-eye steaks
100g hickory smoking chips
2 cups (500ml) water

1 Combine rind, chilli, thyme, paprika, oil and garlic in large bowl with steaks. Cover; refrigerate 3 hours or overnight.
2 Soak chips in the water in medium bowl; stand 3 hours or overnight.
3 Place drained chips in smoke box alongside steaks on grill plate or barbecue. Cook steaks, covered, using indirect heat, about 10 minutes or until cooked.

preparation time 10 minutes
(plus refrigeration and standing time)
cooking time 10 minutes
serves 4
per serving 27.3g fat; 1726kJ (413 cal)
tip The hickory smoking chips called for here are available at most barbecue supply stores, as are other varieties of wood chips that can also be used to smoke meat on the barbecue.

FENNEL-SEASONED STEAK WITH FRIED GREEN TOMATOES

2 teaspoons fennel seeds
1 teaspoon sea salt
½ teaspoon cracked black pepper
⅓ cup (80ml) olive oil
4 beef scotch fillet steaks (800g)
4 large green plum tomatoes (360g)
¼ cup (35g) plain flour
1 egg
2 tablespoons milk
¼ cup (85g) polenta
2 tablespoons american mustard
50g wild rocket

1 Using mortar and pestle, coarsely crush seeds, salt and pepper; stir in half of the oil. Rub fennel mixture into beef.
2 Cut tomatoes into 1.5cm slices. Toss slices in flour; shake away excess flour. Dip slices into combined egg and milk; coat in polenta.
3 Heat remaining oil in large frying pan; cook slices until browned lightly both sides and just tender.
4 Cook beef on heated oiled grill plate (or grill or barbecue) until cooked as desired. Cover beef; stand 5 minutes.
5 Serve steak with tomatoes, mustard and wild rocket.

preparation time 10 minutes
cooking time 15 minutes
serves 4
per serving 25.6g fat; 2554kJ (611 cal)

CHILLI-RUBBED HICKORY-SMOKED STEAK

FENNEL-SEASONED STEAK

A taste of the Deep South 91

Shrimp boats are a comin'...

CAJUN PRAWNS

1 tablespoon hot paprika
1 teaspoon chilli powder
1 teaspoon ground ginger
2 teaspoons ground cumin
1 teaspoon ground cardamom
1 teaspoon ground coriander
1 tablespoon vegetable oil
1 medium red onion (150g), chopped
coarsely
1 clove garlic, crushed
24 uncooked medium king prawns (1kg)
1 teaspoon vegetable oil, extra
1 tablespoon lime juice
1 lime, cut into wedges

1 Blend or process spices, oil, onion and
garlic until mixture forms a paste. Shell
and devein prawns, leaving tails intact.
2 Heat extra oil in large frying pan; cook
prawns, in batches, until just changed in
colour.
3 Cook paste, stirring, in same pan about
2 minutes or until fragrant. Return prawns
to pan with juice; cook until prawns are
heated through.
4 Serve prawns with lime wedges and salad.

preparation time 30 minutes
cooking time 15 minutes
serves 4
per serving 6.6g fat; 740kJ (177 cal)

CHAR-GRILLED PRAWNS WITH MANGO CHILLI SALAD

1kg uncooked large prawns

mango chilli salad
¼ cup (60ml) lime juice
2 fresh small red thai chillies, chopped finely
¼ cup (60ml) olive oil
2 teaspoons sugar
1 medium mango (430g), chopped
1 medium green mango (430g), sliced thinly
1 small red onion (100g), sliced thinly
½ cup firmly packed fresh coriander leaves

1 Make mango chilli salsa.
2 Cook prawns in their shells on heated,
oiled grill plate (or grill or barbecue) until
changed colour and cooked through.
3 Serve prawns with mango chilli salad.

mango chilli salad Combine juice, chilli,
oil and sugar in medium bowl; stir until the
sugar is dissolved. Add mangoes, onion and
coriander; toss gently.

preparation time 15 minutes
cooking time 5 minutes
serves 4
per serving 14.8g fat; 1405kJ (336 cal)

CHAR-GRILLED PRAWNS

FRESH SHRIMP

CRAB, PRAWN & CORN CAKES

LOBSTER TAILS WITH LIME BUTTER

Crab & lobster

CRAB, PRAWN & CORN CAKES

3 medium potatoes (600g), chopped coarsely
300g can corn kernels, drained
200g cooked medium prawns, chopped coarsely
170g can crab meat, drained
⅓ cup finely chopped fresh coriander leaves
1 egg, beaten lightly
1 tablespoon sweet chilli sauce
½ small red onion (50g), chopped finely
40g butter, melted

1 Boil, steam or microwave potatoes until soft; drain. Mash potatoes until smooth; cool.
2 Preheat oven to hot (220°C/200°C fan-assisted).
3 Combine mashed potato, corn, prawns, crab, coriander, egg, sauce and onion in medium bowl.
4 Shape ⅓ cups of mixture into patties; place on oven tray lined with baking parchment; brush with butter. Bake 15 minutes; turn carefully, bake a further 15 minutes or until browned lightly. Serve patties with extra sweet chilli sauce, if desired.

preparation time 20 minutes
cooking time 35 minutes (plus cooling time)
serves 4
per serving 11.1g fat; 1317kJ (315 cal)

LOBSTER TAILS WITH LIME BUTTER & PINEAPPLE MINT SALSA

100g butter
1 teaspoon finely grated lime rind
1 fresh small red thai chilli, chopped finely
2cm piece fresh ginger (10g), grated
4 uncooked small lobster tails in shells (660g)

pineapple mint salsa
1 small pineapple (900g), chopped coarsely
2 tablespoons lime juice
½ cup finely chopped fresh mint
1 fresh long red chilli, chopped finely

1 Combine ingredients for pineapple mint salsa in medium bowl.
2 Melt butter in small saucepan; cook rind, chilli and ginger, stirring, 2 minutes.
3 Using scissors, cut soft shell from underneath lobster tails to expose meat; cut lobster tails in half lengthways. Brush with butter mixture; cook, in batches, on heated oiled grill plate until cooked through. Serve with salsa.

preparation time 20 minutes
cooking time 10 minutes
serves 4
per serving 21.9g fat; 1538kJ (368 cal)

On the side

SOUTHERN-STYLE CABBAGE

2 cups (500ml) water
1 medium onion (150g), chopped finely
1 bay leaf
½ teaspoon allspice
¼ teaspoon ground cumin
2 cloves garlic, crushed
1 tablespoon worcestershire sauce
2 teaspoons tamari
2 teaspoons honey
500g savoy cabbage, sliced thickly
500g red cabbage, sliced thickly
1 tablespoon extra virgin olive oil
½ teaspoon cayenne pepper

1 Combine the water, onion, bay leaf, allspice, cumin, garlic, sauce, tamari and honey in medium saucepan; cover. Bring to a boil; reduce heat. Simmer, uncovered, 5 minutes.
2 Add both cabbages; cook, uncovered, further 5 minutes or until tender, stirring occasionally.
3 Remove bay leaf; stir in oil and pepper.

preparation time 15 minutes
cooking time 25 minutes
serves 4
per serving 5.4g fat; 496kJ (118 cal)

SWEET POTATO SCONES

400g sweet potato, chopped coarsely
⅔ cup (160ml) soy milk
2 teaspoons lemon juice
1 cup (160g) plain wholemeal flour
1 cup (150g) plain flour
1 tablespoon baking powder
1 teaspoon bicarbonate of soda
1 tablespoon raw sugar
½ teaspoon salt
¼ cup (60ml) sunflower oil

1 Preheat oven to hot (220°C/200°C fan-assisted).
2 Boil or steam sweet potato in medium saucepan until tender; drain. Mash; cool.
3 Combine soy milk and juice, stand 10 minutes or until milk thickens slightly (it will resemble buttermilk). Place wholemeal flour in large bowl; add plain flour, baking powder, soda, sugar and salt. Add sweet potato, soy milk and oil; combine to form a soft dough.
4 Turn onto a lightly floured surface; knead until just smooth. Press out until dough is about 3cm thick; cut into 8cm squares.
5 Place squares 1cm apart on baking parchment covered baking tray. Bake 15 minutes or until golden brown, serve warm or cold.

preparation time 30 minutes
(plus standing time)
cooking time 15 minutes
makes 12
per scone 5.6g fat; 679kJ (162 cal)

CAJUN POTATO WEDGES

2kg potatoes, unpeeled
¼ cup (60ml) olive oil
1 teaspoon ground oregano
3 teaspoons ground cumin
2 teaspoons hot paprika
1 teaspoon ground black pepper
2 teaspoons ground turmeric
2 teaspoons ground coriander
½ teaspoon chilli powder

1 Preheat oven to 200°C/180°C fan-assisted. Oil three oven trays.
2 Cut each potato into wedges; toss potato with remaining ingredients in large bowl.
3 Place wedges, in single layer, on trays; roast, uncovered, turning occasionally, about 40 minutes or until crisp and cooked through.

preparation time 10 minutes
cooking time 40 minutes
serves 10
per serving 5.7g fat; 765kJ (183 cal)

CAJUN POTATO WEDGES

SOUTHERN-STYLE CABBAGE WITH SWEET POTATO SCONES

Deep South desserts

HUMMINGBIRD CAKE

450g can crushed pineapple in syrup
1 cup (150g) plain flour
½ cup (75g) self-raising flour
½ teaspoon bicarbonate of soda
½ teaspoon ground cinnamon
½ teaspoon ground ginger
1 cup (220g) firmly packed brown sugar
½ cup (40g) desiccated coconut
1 cup mashed banana
2 eggs, beaten lightly
¾ cup (180ml) vegetable oil

cream cheese frosting
30g butter, softened
60g packaged cream cheese, softened
1 teaspoon vanilla extract
1½ cups (240g) icing sugar

1 Preheat oven to moderate (180°C/160°C
fan-assisted). Grease deep 23cm-square cake
tin; line base with baking parchment.
2 Drain pineapple over a bowl, pressing with
spoon to extract as much syrup as possible.
Reserve ¼ cup syrup.
3 Sift flours, soda, spices and sugar into
large bowl. Stir in pineapple, reserved syrup,
coconut, banana, egg and oil; pour into tin.
Bake about 40 minutes. Stand cake 5 minutes
then turn onto wire rack; cool.
4 Make cream cheese frosting.
5 Spread cold cake with frosting.

cream cheese frosting Beat butter, cream
cheese and extract in small bowl with electric mixer until light and fluffy; gradually
beat in sifted icing sugar.

preparation time 35 minutes
cooking time 40 minutes
serves 12

MISSISSIPPI MUD CAKE

250g butter, chopped
150g dark eating chocolate, chopped
2 cups (440g) caster sugar
1 cup (250ml) hot water
⅓ cup (80ml) coffee-flavoured liqueur
1 tablespoon instant coffee powder
1½ cups (225g) plain flour
¼ cup (35g) self-raising flour
¼ cup (25g) cocoa powder
2 eggs, beaten lightly

1 Preheat oven to moderately low. Grease
deep 20cm-round cake tin; line base and side
with baking parchment.
2 Combine butter, chocolate, sugar, the
water, liqueur and coffee powder in medium
saucepan. Using wooden spoon, stir over low
heat until chocolate melts.
3 Transfer mixture to large bowl; cool
15 minutes. Whisk in combined sifted flours
and cocoa powder, then egg. Pour mixture
into prepared tin.
4 Bake about 1½ hours. Stand cake in tin
30 minutes before turning onto wire rack;
turn cake top-side up to cool.

preparation time 25 minutes
(plus cooling time)
cooking time 1 hour 35 minutes
serves 10

MISSISSIPPI MUD CAKE

Hummingbird cake, a moist, luscious cake made with crushed pineapple and mashed banana, was created in the American south, where ladies' lunches and afternoon teas were once a way of life. It will keep for several days in an airtight container.

HUMMINGBIRD CAKE

KEY LIME PIE

BLACK BOTTOM PIE

The key lime flourishes in Florida, where it is used in many dishes. In this famous recipe, a reaction occurs between the condensed milk and the lime juice causing the filling to thicken.
Black Bottom pie comes from Kentucky. Its name comes simply from the fact that the base layer of filling is chocolate.

KEY LIME PIE

1 cup (150g) plain flour
2 teaspoons icing sugar
60g butter
2 teaspoons lemon juice
1 tablespoon water, approximately

filling
¾ cup (185 ml) sweetened condensed milk
1 cup (200g) ricotta cheese
3 eggs, separated
2 teaspoons finely grated lemon rind
⅓ cup (80ml) lime juice

1 Sift flour and icing sugar into bowl, rub in butter. Stir in lemon juice and enough water to mix to a soft dough. Knead gently on floured surface until smooth; cover, refrigerate 30 minutes. Preheat oven to moderately hot (200°C/180°C fan-assisted).
2 Roll dough between sheets of baking parchment until large enough to fit 23cm pie plate. Ease pastry into pie plate; trim edge.
3 Place pie plate on oven tray, line pastry with baking parchment, then fill with dried beans or uncooked rice. Bake 10 minutes. Remove paper and beans; bake, uncovered, 7 minutes or until browned lightly. Cool.
4 Make filling. Pour into pastry case; bake about 25 minutes or until filling is set. Cool.
5 Refrigerate pie until cold; dust with sifted icing sugar before serving, if desired.

filling Blend or process milk, cheese, yolks, rind and juice until smooth; transfer to large bowl. Beat egg whites in small bowl to soft peaks, fold into lime mixture in two batches.

preparation time 20 minutes
(plus refrigeration time)
cooking time 35 minutes
serves 8

BLACK BOTTOM PIE

1 sheet ready-rolled sweet shortcrust pastry
½ cup whipping cream, whipped
30g dark chocolate, grated

filling
1 tablespoon gelatine
¼ cup milk + 1 cup milk, extra
¼ cup caster sugar
3 teaspoons cornflour
3 eggs, separated
60g dark chocolate, melted
1 teaspoon vanilla essence
¼ cup caster sugar, extra

1 Unroll pastry on floured surface and use to line a 23cm pie plate. Trim edge; prick pastry all over with a fork.
3 Bake in moderately hot oven 15 minutes or until browned; cool.
4 Spread chocolate custard into pastry case; chill until firm. Top with vanilla custard; chill until firm. Spread whipped cream over custard, then sprinkle with extra chocolate.

filling Sprinkle gelatine over milk in cup. Blend sugar and cornflour with extra milk in pan; stir over heat until mixture boils and thickens, remove from heat. Quickly stir in yolks, then gelatine mixture; stir until smooth. Divide custard into 2 bowls. Stir chocolate into 1 bowl. Cover both bowls; cool. Stir essence into plain custard. Beat egg whites in small bowl with electric mixer to soft peaks; gradually add extra sugar, beating until dissolved after additions. Fold egg whites into vanilla custard in 2 batches.

preparation time 20 minutes
(plus refrigeration time)
cooking time 20 minutes
serves 6 to 8

Southern coolers

MINT JULEP

30ml mint syrup (see below)
60ml bourbon
2 cups ice cubes

1 Pour 10ml of the mint syrup into a chilled glass. Combine bourbon and ice in jug of a blender, blend until smooth.
2 Spoon bourbon mixture into glass; stir, drizzle with remaining mint syrup.

makes 1
tip This cocktail should be made with the best bourbon you can buy.

MINT SYRUP

2 cups firmly packed fresh mint leaves
1 quantity sugar syrup (see opposite)

1 Fill a large bowl with ice and water. Bring a small pan of water to a boil. Plunge mint into boiling water for about 3 seconds. Remove with a slotted spoon and immediately transfer to iced water until cold; drain.
2 Combine sugar syrup and mint in a blender jug; blend until pureed, stand syrup for 10 minutes. Push syrup through a fine sieve, pressing down firmly to extract as much liquid from mint as possible, discard mint pulp. Store in an airtight container for up to 1 week in the refrigerator.

makes about 180ml

PLANTER'S PUNCH

1 cup ice cubes
50ml Bacardi
25ml fresh lime juice
20ml lime juice cordial
dash Angostura bitters
30ml soda water

1 Combine ice, Bacardi, juice, cordial and bitters in a cocktail shaker.
2 Shake vigorously, then pour mixture into a glass; top with chilled soda water, stir.

makes 1

CAJUN BLOODY MARY

1 cup ice cubes
30ml chilli-infused vodka
10ml fresh lemon juice
dash worcestershire sauce
dash tabasco sauce
pinch celery salt
pinch cracked black pepper
120ml tomato juice

1 Combine ice, vodka, lemon juice and sauces in glass rimmed (see page 70) with celery salt and pepper; add tomato juice, stir.
2 Garnish with lemon wedges

makes 1
tip To make chilli-infused vodka, combine 250ml vodka and 4 fresh red thai chillies in a glass jar, cover; stand for about 5 days. Discard chillies before use.

MINYT JULEP

CAJUN BLOODY MARY

Sugar syrup

Sugar syrup, often called gomme syrup, is used for sweetening drinks: Combine ½ cup (110g) sugar and ½ cup (125ml) water in a small pan; stir over low heat until sugar dissolves. Bring to a boil, then reduce heat and simmer, uncovered, without stirring, 5 minutes; remove from heat, cool (makes about 350ml).

Diner specials

The American diner has its origins in horse-drawn lunch wagons that used to supply workers with hot food in the late 19th century. The original diner was long and narrow, built to allow for road transport. Though they were never intended to stay in one place, many ended life on the railroad – when a dining car was no longer fit for service, it was often used as a cheap restaurant near a train station or along the side of the road. Diners tend to serve classic American fast food – hamburgers, sandwiches, milkshakes and of course the ubiquitous all-day breakfast!

All-day breakfast

BAGELS WITH SCRAMBLED EGGS & SMOKED SALMON

2 eggs, beaten lightly
10 egg whites
2 tablespoons finely chopped fresh chives
2 bagels
½ cucumber (130g), sliced thinly
200g sliced smoked salmon

1 Whisk eggs, whites and chives together in medium bowl. Heat oiled medium pan, add egg mixture, gently stir over low heat until almost set.
2 Split bagels in half; toast both sides. Top bagel halves with cucumber, eggs and smoked salmon.

preparation time 10 minutes
cooking time 5 minutes
serves 4
per serving 7g fat; 1217kJ (291 cal)

SCRAMBLED EGGS & BACON

250g cherry tomatoes
1 tablespoon olive oil
8 slices thin bacon (240g)
8 eggs
½ cup (125ml) double cream
2 tablespoons finely chopped fresh chives
30g butter
4 slices crusty bread, toasted

1 Preheat grill. Toss tomatoes in oil. Cook bacon and tomato under grill until bacon is crisp and tomato skins start to split. Cover to keep warm.
2 Meanwhile, combine eggs, cream and chives in bowl; beat lightly with fork.
3 Heat butter in large frying pan over medium heat. Add egg mixture, wait a few seconds, then use a wide spatula to gently scrape the set egg mixture along the base of the pan; cook until creamy and just set.
4 Serve toast topped with egg, bacon and tomatoes.

preparation time 10 minutes
cooking time 15 minutes
serves 4
per serving 52g fat; 3223kJ (771 cal)

SCRAMBLED EGGS & BACON

Special BREAK 3 EGG 3 EG

THANK YOU

Coffee

EST RECEIPT

Date

CINNAMON TOAST

3 eggs, beaten lightly
⅓ cup (80ml) double cream
⅓ cup (80ml) milk
¼ teaspoon ground cinnamon
1 tablespoon caster sugar
12 x 2cm slices french bread stick
50g butter

1 Combine egg, cream, milk, cinnamon and sugar in large bowl. Dip bread slices into egg mixture.
2 Melt half the butter in large frying pan; cook half the bread slices until browned both sides. Repeat with remaining butter and bread.
3 Serve cinnamon toast sprinkled with sifted icing sugar, if desired.

preparation time 5 minutes
cooking time 10 minutes
serves 4
per serving 24.8g fat; 1450kJ (347 cal)

CINNAMON TOAST

FRENCH TOAST WITH BLUEBERRY COMPOTE

4 eggs
½ cup (125ml) double cream
¼ cup (60ml) milk
1 teaspoon finely grated orange rind
1 teaspoon ground cinnamon
¼ cup (90g) honey
100g butter, melted
8 thick slices sourdough bread (560g)
¼ cup (40g) icing sugar

blueberry compote
1 teaspoon arrowroot
⅓ cup (80ml) water
2 cups (300g) frozen blueberries
2 tablespoons caster sugar
1 tablespoon finely grated orange rind

1 Whisk eggs, cream, milk, rind, cinnamon and honey in large bowl until combined.
2 Make blueberry compote.
3 Heat a quarter of the butter in medium frying pan. Dip two bread slices into egg mixture; cook until browned both sides. Remove from pan; cover to keep warm. Repeat with remaining ingredients.
3 Dust french toast with sifted icing sugar; serve with warm blueberry compote.

blueberry compote Blend arrowroot with the water in small saucepan until smooth. Stir in remaining ingredients; cook until mixture almost boils and thickens slightly.

preparation time 15 minutes
cooking time 10 minutes
serves 4
per serving 43.7g fat; 3787kj (906cal)

POACHED EGGS ON SOURDOUGH BREAD

4 eggs
8 slices thin bacon (120g)
50g baby spinach leaves
½ loaf sourdough bread (335g)

1 Preheat grill.
2 Half-fill large shallow frying pan with water; bring to a boil. Break eggs into cup, one at a time, then slide into pan. When all eggs are in pan, allow water to return to a boil. Cover pan, turn off heat; stand about 4 minutes or until a light film sets over yolks. Remove eggs, one at a time, using slotted spoon; place spoon on absorbent-paper-lined saucer briefly to blot up any liquid.

3 Meanwhile, cook bacon, in single layer, under preheated grill.
4 Boil, steam or microwave spinach until just wilted; drain. Using hand, squeeze excess water from spinach.
5 Meanwhile, trim end from bread; cut into four slices. Toast bread both sides; divide among serving plates. Top each with 1 slice bacon, a quarter of the spinach and an egg, then top with second slice bacon.

preparation time 5 minutes
cooking time 15 minutes
serves 4
per serving 9.2g fat; 1313kJ (314 cal)

BACON & CORN SOUFFLÉ OMELETTE

The denver omelette is called a 'western' in most states east of the Mississippi and a 'denver' in the western half of the USA. It's believed to have developed from the egg foo yung served by Chinese cooks to the work gangs building the east-to-west-coast railway in the 1840s. Today, the denver is often served doused in tomato sauce and eaten between slices of white bread.

BACON & CORN SOUFFLÉ OMELETTE

3 rindless bacon rashers (195g), chopped finely
1 clove garlic, crushed
½ medium red pepper (100g), chopped finely
3 spring onions, chopped finely
125g can corn kernels, drained
6 eggs, separated
1 tablespoon water
20g butter
½ cup (60g) finely grated gruyère cheese

1 Cook bacon in oiled omelette pan until crisp. Add garlic, pepper, onion and corn; cook, stirring, until softened. Remove from heat; cover to keep warm.
2 Lightly beat yolks and the water in large bowl until combined. Beat egg whites in medium bowl with electric mixer until soft peaks form; fold into yolks, in two batches.
3 Meanwhile, melt half of the butter in same pan. Pour half of the egg mixture into pan, smooth top. Cook over medium heat until browned underneath. If necessary, cover pan handle with foil, then place pan under preheated grill until top is just set.
4 Spoon half of the corn mixture over omelette, sprinkle with half of the cheese. Fold in half; slide onto serving plate. Repeat with remaining butter, egg, corn mixture and cheese.

preparation time 15 minutes
cooking time 10 minutes
serves 2
per serving 41.7g fat; 2483kJ (594 cal)

DENVER OMELETTE

10 eggs
⅓ cup (80g) soured cream
2 fresh small red chillies, chopped finely
2 teaspoons vegetable oil
1 green pepper (200g), chopped finely
3 spring onions, sliced thinly
100g ham, chopped finely
2 small tomatoes (180g), deseeded, chopped
½ cup (60g) coarsely grated cheddar cheese

1 Whisk eggs lightly in large bowl; whisk in sour cream and chilli.
2 Heat oil in omelette pan; cook pepper and onion, stirring, until onion softens. Place onion mixture in medium bowl with ham, tomato and cheese; stir gently to combine.
3 Pour ¼ cup of the egg mixture into same omelette pan; cook, tilting pan, over low heat until almost set. Sprinkle about ⅓ cup of the filling over half of the omelette; using spatula, fold omelette over to cover the filling.
4 Pour ¼ cup of the egg mixture into empty half of pan; cook over low heat until almost set. Sprinkle about ⅓ cup of the filling over folded omelette, fold omelette over top of first omelette to cover filling. Repeat twice more, using ¼ cup of the egg mixture each time, to form one large layered omelette. Carefully slide omelette onto plate; cover to keep warm.
5 Repeat steps 3 and 4 to make second omelette, using remaining egg mixture and filling. Cut each denver omelette in half.

preparation time 10 minutes
cooking time 15 minutes
serves 4
per serving 30.2g fat; 1639kJ (392 cal)

STRAWBERRY HOTCAKES WITH BLUEBERRY SAUCE

1 egg, separated
½ cup (125ml) apple sauce
1 teaspoon vanilla extract
2 cups (560g) low-fat natural yogurt
1¾ cups (260g) wholemeal self-raising flour
250g strawberries, hulled, chopped coarsely
2 egg whites, extra

blueberry sauce
150g blueberries, chopped coarsely
2 tablespoons white sugar
1 tablespoon water

1 Make blueberry sauce.
2 Combine egg yolk, apple sauce, extract, yogurt, flour and strawberries in large bowl.
3 Using electric mixer, beat all egg whites in small bowl until soft peaks form. Fold egg whites into yogurt mixture.
4 Pour ¼-cup batter into heated large lightly greased non-stick frying pan; using spatula, spread batter to shape into a round. Cook, over low heat, until bubbles appear on the surface. Turn hotcake; cook until browned lightly on other side. Remove from pan; cover to keep warm. Repeat with remaining batter. Serve with blueberry sauce.

blueberry sauce Combine ingredients in small saucepan; bring to a boil, stirring constantly. Reduce heat; simmer 2 minutes. Remove from heat; cool. Blend or process blueberry mixture until smooth.

preparation time 15 minutes
cooking time 20 minutes
serves 4
per serving 3.2g fat; 1735kJ (415 cal)

BUCKWHEAT PANCAKES WITH LEMON CREAM

½ cup (75g) buckwheat flour
¼ cup (35g) wholemeal self-raising flour
1½ teaspoons baking powder
½ teaspoon ground cinnamon
2 egg whites
¾ cup (180ml) skimmed milk
1 tablespoon lemon juice
2 tablespoons maple syrup
20g low-fat dairy-free spread, melted
2 teaspoons coarsely grated lemon rind

lemon cream
⅓ cup (80g) light soured cream
1 teaspoon finely grated lemon rind
1 teaspoon caster sugar

1 Sift flours, baking powder and cinnamon into medium bowl; gradually whisk in combined egg white, milk, juice and syrup. Stir spread into batter.
2 Pour ¼ cup batter into heated small lightly greased non-stick frying pan; cook about 2 minutes or until bubbles appear on the surface. Turn pancake; cook until lightly browned on other side. Remove from pan; cover to keep warm. Repeat with remaining batter. Serve pancakes with lemon cream; top with grated lemon rind.

lemon cream Place ingredients in small bowl; stir until combined.

preparation time 10 minutes
cooking time 10 minutes
serves 4
per serving 6g fat; 837kJ (200 cal)

Banana sauce

As a delicious alternative sauce for your pancakes: melt 90g butter in a pan, add ¾ cup firmly packed brown sugar; stir over medium heat about 1 minute or until sugar is dissolved. Stir in ¾ cup double cream and ½ cup soured cream. Add 4 thickly sliced bananas and 2 table-spoons toasted shredded coconut; stir gently.

STRAWBERRY HOTCAKES WITH BLUEBERRY SAUCE

BUCKWHEAT PANCAKES WITH LEMON CREAM

Waffles

WAFFLES WITH CARAMEL SAUCE

1¾ cups (265g) plain flour
¼ cup (35g) self-raising flour
¼ cup (55g) caster sugar
2 eggs, separated
1½ cups (375ml) milk
60g butter, melted
2 tablespoons water

caramel sauce
125g butter
1 cup (220g) firmly packed brown sugar
300ml double cream

1 Make caramel sauce.
2 Sift flours and sugar into medium bowl. Make well in centre, gradually stir in combined egg yolks and milk, then butter and water; stir until smooth.
3 Beat egg whites in small bowl with electric mixer until soft peaks form; fold into batter, in two batches.
4 Preheat waffle iron. Drop about ⅓ cup of mixture onto heated oiled waffle iron. Close iron; cook about 2 minutes or until golden brown. Repeat with remaining batter.
5 5 Serve waffles with caramel sauce and ice-cream, if desired.

caramel sauce Melt butter in medium saucepan, add sugar; stir over heat, without boiling, until sugar is dissolved. Bring to a boil; simmer, without stirring, 2 minutes. Remove from heat, allow bubbles to subside, stir in cream.

preparation time 15 minutes
cooking time 10 minutes
serves 6
per serving 48.7g fat; 3453kJ (826 cal)

CARAMELISED BANANA & PECAN WAFFLES

4 packaged waffles (320g)
40g butter
4 medium ripe bananas (800g), sliced thickly
2 tablespoons caster sugar
½ cup (60g) roasted pecans, chopped coarsely
⅓ cup (80ml) pure maple syrup

1 Preheat oven to moderately low (170°C/ 150°C fan-assisted). Place waffles, in single layer, on oven tray; heat about 8 minutes.
2 Meanwhile, melt butter in medium frying pan; cook banana, stirring, about 2 minutes or until hot. Add sugar; cook, uncovered, over low heat, about 2 minutes or until banana is caramelised lightly.
3 Divide waffles among serving plates; top with banana mixture, nuts and syrup.

preparation time 10 minutes
cooking time 15 minutes
serves 4
per serving 33.9g fat; 2939kj (703 cal)
tip To balance the sweetness of this recipe combine 300g Greek-style yogurt with 1 tablespoon brown sugar and ½ teaspoon vanilla extract, mixing well. Spoon over the waffles.

WAFFLES WITH MAPLE SYRUP & STRAWBERRIES

8 packaged Belgian-style waffles (400g)
20g butter
500g strawberries, hulled, sliced thickly
½ cup (125ml) pure maple syrup

1 Preheat oven to moderately low (170°C/150°C fan-assisted).
2 Place waffles, in single layer, on oven tray; heat, in oven, about 8 minutes.
3 Meanwhile, melt butter in medium frying pan; cook strawberries, stirring gently, about 2 minutes or until just heated through. Add maple syrup; cook, stirring gently, until heated through.
4 Divide waffles among serving plates; top with strawberry maple mixture.

preparation time 15 minutes
cooking time 10 minutes
serves 4
per waffle 22.8g fat; 2316kJ (554 cal)

Sandwiches

BLT, ITALIAN DELI-STYLE

4 medium plum tomatoes (300g), quartered
1 tablespoon balsamic vinegar
1 tablespoon finely chopped fresh basil
¼ cup (60ml) olive oil
8 slices pancetta (120g)
1 loaf ciabatta (440g)
1 clove garlic, crushed
100g mozzarella, sliced thickly
25g baby rocket leaves

1 Place tomatoes in medium bowl with vinegar, basil and 1 tablespoon of the oil; toss tomatoes to coat in mixture.
2 Cook tomato and pancetta on heated oiled grill plate (or grill or barbecue) until tomato is browned and pancetta crisp.
3 Cut bread into quarters, split quarters in half horizontally; brush cut sides with combined garlic and remaining oil. Toast bread, cut-side down, on same grill plate.
4 Sandwich tomato, pancetta, mozzarella and rocket between bread pieces.

preparation time 15 minutes
cooking time 15 minutes
serves 4
per serving 24.5g fat; 2149kj (514 cal)

SPICED BEEF SANDWICH

500g beef rump steak, sliced thinly
1 medium (150g) onion, sliced thinly
1 medium (200g) red pepper, sliced thinly
2 tablespoons cajun seasoning
3 medium (570g) tomatoes
1 long french bread stick

1 Heat oiled large pan; cook beef, in batches, until beef is browned and cooked as desired. Add onion, pepper and seasoning to same pan; cook, stirring, until onion is browned lightly. Cut each tomato into 8 wedges, add to pan; simmer, uncovered, about 15 minutes or until mixture thickens. Return beef to pan; toss gently to combine with tomato mixture.
2 Trim ends from bread stick; quarter stick then split pieces almost all the way through. Line bread with lettuce leaves, if desired. Divide beef mixture among bread pieces just before serving.

preparation time 15 minutes
cooking time 25 minutes
serves 4
per serving 6.1g fat; 1620kJ
(excluding lettuce)

BLT, ITALIAN DELI-STYLE

SPICED BEEF SANDWICH

The BLT (bacon, lettuce and tomato) is said to be the second most popular sandwich in the United States, beaten only by the hamburger. The sandwich traditionally has strips of crispy bacon, iceberg lettuce and slices of tomato set between slices of toasted bread – mayonnaise being the traditional accompaniment.

Bagels & melts

HAM, CHEESE & TOMATO MELT

Spread 2 teaspoons tomato chutney on each of two slices of white bread; top each slice of bread with half a slice of ham, a quarter of a thinly sliced tomato, and one slice of swiss cheese. Place under preheated grill about 5 minutes or until cheese melts.

makes 2
per melt 7.1g fat; 699kJ (167 cal)

SALMON & CUCUMBER BAGEL

Discard skin and bones from a quarter of a drained 210g can red salmon. Combine salmon in small bowl with an eighth of a finely chopped cucumber, 1 teaspoon lemon juice and 1 tablespoon soured cream. Spread 1 tablespoon cream cheese on half of a bagel; top with salmon mixture.

makes 1
per bagel 18.5g fat; 1523kJ (364 cal)

TURKEY MELT

Slice 10cm piece french bread stick in half horizontally; top each half with one slice of smoked turkey breast, a quarter of a thinly sliced green pepper, and one slice of edam cheese. Place under preheated grill about 5 minutes or until cheese melts.

makes 2
per melt 6.8g fat; 653kJ (156 cal)

TUNA MAYO MELT

Combine half a drained 185g can tuna in brine, 2 tablespoons mayonnaise, half of a finely chopped small red onion, and 2 tablespoons finely chopped fresh flat-leaf parsley in small bowl. Cut a 300g garlic focaccia into quarters; spread tuna mixture over one quarter, top with one slice of cheddar cheese. Place under preheated grill about 5 minutes or until cheese melts.

makes 1
per melt 23.9g fat; 2160kJ (516 cal)

SALAMI & TOMATO BAGEL

Spread half a bagel with 1 teaspoon butter; layer with two slices of danish salami, half of a thinly sliced medium plum tomato, 1 tablespoon sliced pitted black olives, and 1 tablespoon coarsely grated pizza cheese.

makes 1
per bagel 11.8g fat; 991kJ (237 cal)

AVOCADO BAGEL MELT

Split bagel in half horizontally; spread 2 teaspoons salsa over each half. Top each half of bagel with a quarter of a thickly sliced small avocado and one slice of cheddar cheese. Place under preheated grill about 5 minutes or until cheese melts.

makes 2
per melt 15.7g fat; 1182kJ (282 cal)

HAM, CHEESE & TOMATO MELT

TUNA MAYO MELT

SALMON & CUCUMBER BAGEL

SALAMI & TOMATO BAGEL

TURKEY MELT

MEXICAN BAGEL MELT

Grill plate specials

GOURMET BURGER

750g minced beef
1 cup (70g) stale breadcrumbs
2 tablespoons finely chopped fresh
flat-leaf parsley
2 tablespoons tomato paste
125g cheddar cheese, sliced thinly
½ cup (150g) mayonnaise
4 bread rolls
50g mixed salad leaves
1 small red onion (100g), sliced thinly
2 tablespoons drained, sliced sun-dried
tomatoes in oil

1 Combine beef, breadcrumbs, parsley
and 1½ tablespoons of the paste in large
bowl. Using hands, shape mixture into four
burgers.
2 Cook burgers on heated oiled barbecue,
uncovered, until browned and cooked
through. Top burgers with cheese; cook
until cheese melts.
3 Combine remaining paste and mayonnaise
in small bowl.
4 Split rolls in half. Place cut-side down onto
barbecue; cook until lightly toasted.
5 Sandwich burgers, mayonnaise mixture,
salad leaves, onion and sliced tomatoes
between bread rolls.

preparation time 15 minutes
cooking time 10 minutes
serves 4
per serving 39.2g fat; 3219kJ (769 cal)

PORK CHUTNEY BURGER

500g minced pork
1 cup (100g) packaged breadcrumbs
1 egg, beaten lightly
1 tablespoon finely chopped fresh
flat-leaf parsley
2 tablespoons fruit chutney
2 tablespoons grated cheddar cheese
4 hamburger buns
2 lettuce leaves, shredded
1 medium tomato (190g), sliced thinly
4 canned pineapple rings

1 Combine pork, breadcrumbs, egg and
parsley in medium bowl. Using hands, shape
mixture into four burgers; flatten slightly.
Indent centres; spoon combined chutney
and cheese into centre of each burger. Shape
burgers around chutney mixture to enclose
mixture; flatten slightly.
2 Cook burgers on heated oiled barbecue,
uncovered, until browned and cooked
through.
3 Split buns in half. Place cut-side down onto
barbecue; cook until lightly toasted.
4 Top base of buns with lettuce, tomato,
pineapple and burgers; top with extra
chutney, if desired. Replace top of buns.

preparation time 20 minutes
cooking time 10 minutes
serves 4
per serving 14.6g fat; 2096kJ (501 cal)

GOURMET BURGER

WIENERBURGER
AIRCONDITIONED
DINER
CURB SERVICE
IN SUMMER

Hamburgers don't often contain ham – the term originally derives from the German town of Hamburg, from where many emigrants came to America.

'Anybody who doesn't think that the best hamburger place in the world is in his home town is a sissy.'

Calvin Trillin

PORK CHUTNEY BURGER

CHILLI BURGER

750g minced beef
310g can red kidney beans, rinsed, drained
4 spring onions, chopped finely
2 fresh red thai chillies, deseeded, chopped finely
1 teaspoon hot paprika
1 tablespoon tomato paste
6 hamburger buns
6 round lettuce leaves
1 small avocado (200g), mashed
½ cup (120g) soured cream
2 tablespoons lemon juice

1 Combine beef, beans, onion, chilli, paprika and paste in medium bowl. Using hands, shape mixture into six burgers.
2 Cook burgers on heated oiled barbecue until well browned and cooked through
3 Split buns in half. Place cut-side down onto barbecue; cook until lightly toasted.
4 Top base of buns with lettuce, burgers and combined avocado, soured cream, and juice. Replace top of buns, if desired

preparation time 20 minutes
cooking time 10 minutes
serves 6
per serving 26.9g fat; 2090kJ (499 cal)

BURGERS WITH MUSTARD MAYO

500g minced beef
½ cup (40g) packaged stuffing mix
½ cup (60ml) tomato sauce
¼ cup coarsely chopped flat-leaf parsley
2 large white onions (400g), sliced thinly
4 hamburger buns
8 oak leaf lettuce leaves
1 large tomato (250g), sliced thinly
1 tablespoon american mustard
½ cup (150g) mayonnaise

1 Combine beef, stuffing mix, sauce and parsley in medium bowl. Using hands, shape mixture into four burgers.
2 Cook burgers on heated oiled barbecue, uncovered, until browned and cooked through.
3 Meanwhile, cook onion on heated oiled barbecue plate until soft and browned.
4 Split buns in half. Place cut-side down onto barbecue; cook until lightly toasted.
5 Top base of buns with lettuce, tomato, patties, combined mustard and mayonnaise, then onion; replace top of buns.

preparation time 20 minutes
cooking time 15 minutes
serves 4
per serving 26.6g fat; 2322kJ (555 cal)

BURGERS WITH MUSTARD MAYO

CHILLI BURGER

NEW YORK STRIPS

ULTIMATE STEAK SANDWICH

ULTIMATE STEAK SANDWICH

2 tablespoons vegetable oil
2 large red onions (600g), sliced thinly
1 tablespoon brown sugar
2 tablespoons balsamic vinegar
200g chestnut mushrooms, sliced thinly
4 x 200g beef scotch fillet steaks
8 thick slices ciabatta (360g)
100g liver pâté
¼ cup (70g) american mustard
40g baby rocket leaves

1 Heat half the oil on grill plate; cook onion, turning constantly, until browned lightly. Sprinkle onion with sugar and vinegar; cook, turning constantly, until onion is caramelised. Transfer onion to small bowl; cover to keep warm.
2 Heat remaining oil on grill plate; cook mushrooms, turning, until browned and tender.
3 Meanwhile, cook steaks on grill plate until cooked. Cover; stand while toasting bread, both sides, on grill plate.
4 Sandwich pâté, mustard, rocket, mushrooms, steak and onion between slices of bread.

preparation time 20 minutes
cooking time 40 minutes
serves 4
per serving 32.8g fat; 4025kJ (963 cal)

NEW YORK STRIPS WITH LEMON THYME BUTTER

4 large potatoes (1.2kg), cut into wedges
2 medium red onions (340g), cut into wedges
1 medium lemon (140g), cut into wedges
2 teaspoons fresh thyme leaves
¼ cup (60ml) olive oil
4 New York-cut beef steaks (880g)

lemon thyme butter
60g butter, softened
2 teaspoons finely grated lemon rind
1 teaspoon finely chopped fresh thyme
1 clove garlic, crushed

1 Preheat oven to hot (220°C/200°C fan-assisted).
2 Make lemon thyme butter.
3 Combine potato, onion, lemon, thyme and oil in large deep baking dish. Bake, uncovered, in hot oven, stirring occasionally, about 45 minutes or until potato is browned and crisp.
4 Meanwhile, cook beef, in batches, on heated, oiled grill plate (or grill or barbecue) until browned both sides and cooked as desired.
5 Serve beef with potato and onion mixture, topped with lemon thyme butter.

lemon thyme butter Combine ingredients in small bowl. Cover; refrigerate until firm.

preparation time 15 minutes
(plus refrigeration time)
cooking time 45 minutes
serves 4
per serving 46.4g fat; 3306kJ (791 cal)
tip New York-cut steaks are also known as porterhouse or boneless sirloin steaks.

Side order of potatoes

ROSEMARY & GARLIC WEDGES

Preheat oven to moderately hot. Cut 1kg unpeeled salad potatoes into wedges. Combine in bowl with 6 chopped rosemary sprigs, 2 tablespoons olive oil and 2 crushed garlic cloves. Roast wedges on oven tray in hot oven about 40 minutes or until tender.

preparation time 10 minutes
cooking time 40 minutes
serves 4
per serving 9.4g fat; 1066kJ (255 cal)

BLUE-CHEESE BAKED POTATOES

Pierce 4 large unpeeled potatoes with fork; wrap in foil. Cook potatoes in hot oven about 1 hour until tender. Grill 60g thin cur bacon until crisp. Cut cross in potatoes; squeeze with tongs to open. Divide combined ¾ cup soured cream and 50g crumbled blue cheese among potatoes, sprinkle with crumbled bacon pieces.

preparation time 10 minutes
cooking time 1 hour
serves 4
per serving 24g fat; 1877kJ (449 cal);

SWEET POTATO SLICES

Cut 2 large sweet potatoes into 1cm slices; boil until tender, drain. Cook sweet potatoes on heated oiled grill plate until browned; turn, brush with combined 1 crushed garlic clove, 2 tablespoons golden syrup, 2 teaspoons balsamic vinegar and ¼ teaspoon ground cinnamon.

preparation time 15 minutes
cooking time 25 minutes
serves 6
per serving 0.2g fat; 443kJ (106 cal)

HASH BROWNS

Thinly slice 1 large onion. Coarsely grate 1kg floury potatoes; stir in 1 teaspoon salt. Squeeze moisture from potato. Mix in onion; cook a quarter of the mixture at a time on heated oiled flat plate or heavy-based frying pan, turning until browned.

preparation time 10 minutes
cooking time 15 minutes
serves 4
per serving 0.3g fat; 711kJ (170 cal)

BLUE CHEESE BAKED POTATOES

HASH BROWNS

ROSEMARY & GARLIC WEDGES

BARBECUED SWEET POTATOES

A slice of pie

BANOFFEE PIE

395g can sweetened condensed milk
80g butter, chopped
½ cup (110g) firmly packed brown sugar
2 tablespoons golden syrup
2 large bananas (460g), sliced thinly
300ml whipping cream, whipped

pastry
1½ cups (225g) plain flour
1 tablespoon icing sugar
140g chilled butter, chopped
1 egg yolk
2 tablespoons iced water, approximately

1 Grease 24cm-round loose-based fluted flan tin. Make pastry.
2 Roll dough between sheets of baking parchment until large enough to line tin. Ease dough into tin. Trim edge; prick base all over with fork. Cover; refrigerate 30 minutes.
3 Preheat oven to 200°C/180°C fan-assisted.
4 Place tin on oven tray; line pastry with baking parchment, fill with dried beans or rice. Bake 10 minutes. Remove paper and beans; bake further 10 minutes. Cool.
5 Meanwhile, combine milk, butter, sugar and syrup in pan; stir over medium heat 10 minutes or until mixture is caramel-coloured. Stand 5 minutes; pour into pie shell, cool.
6 Top with banana then whipped cream.

pastry Process flour, sugar and butter until crumbly. Add egg yolk and the water; process until ingredients come together. Knead dough on floured surface until smooth. Wrap in cling film; refrigerate 30 minutes.

preparation time 45 minutes (plus refrigeration time)
cooking time 35 minutes
serves 10

LEMON CHIFFON PIE

250g digestive biscuits
125g butter, melted
4 eggs, separated
⅓ cup (75g) caster sugar
3 teaspoons gelatine
2 teaspoons finely grated lemon rind
⅓ cup (80ml) lemon juice
⅓ cup (80ml) water
⅓ cup (75g) caster sugar, extra

1 Grease deep 23cm pie dish.
2 Process biscuits until fine; add butter, process until combined. Press mixture over base and side of dish. Chill 30 minutes.
3 Combine yolks, sugar, gelatine, rind, juice and the water in medium heatproof bowl. Whisk over medium saucepan of simmering water until mixture thickens slightly. Remove from heat; pour into large bowl. Cover; cool.
4 Beat egg whites in small bowl with electric mixer to soft peaks; gradually add extra sugar, beating until sugar dissolves. Fold egg mixture into filling mixture, in two batches.
5 Spread filling into crumb crust; refrigerate 3 hours before serving.

preparation time 20 minutes (plus refrigeration time)
cooking time 15 minutes
serves 6

'A la mode...'

To serve your slice of pie 'à la mode',
simply add a scoop or two of vanilla
ice-cream.

Ice-cream sundaes

MOCHA LIQUEUR SUNDAE

100g dark eating chocolate
⅔ cup (160ml) whipping cream
1 tablespoon coffee-flavoured liqueur
1 litre chocolate ice-cream
150g chocolate-coated coffee beans

1 Stir chocolate and cream in medium pan, over low heat, until mixture is smooth; stir in liqueur. Cool 10 minutes.
2 Layer ice-cream chocolate sauce and coffee beans in four serving glasses.

preparation time 5 minutes
cooking time 5 minutes
serves 4

SUMMER BERRY SUNDAE

¼ cup (55g) caster sugar
500g mixed frozen mixed berries
1 tablespoon orange-flavoured liqueur
1 litre vanilla ice-cream
⅔ cup (100g) toasted macadamias, chopped

1 Stir sugar and berries in medium pan over heat, without boiling, until sugar dissolves; bring to a boil. Reduce heat; simmer, uncovered, about 5 minutes or until berries soften. Stir in liqueur; cool 10 minutes.
2 Layer ice-cream, berry mixture and nuts in four serving glasses.

preparation time 5 minutes
cooking time 15 minutes
serves 4

LEMON MERINGUE SUNDAE

⅔ cup (220g) lemon curd
⅓ cup (80ml) double cream
1 litre vanilla ice-cream
4 mini meringues (40g), chopped coarsely

1 Stir lemon curd and cream in small pan, over low heat, until smooth; cool 10 minutes.
2 Layer ice-cream, lemon curd mixture and meringue in four serving glasses.

preparation time 5 minutes
cooking time 5 minutes
serves 4

BANANA CARAMEL SUNDAE

⅔ cup (160ml) whipping cream
60g butter
¾ cup (165g) firmly packed brown sugar
1 cup (250ml) whipping cream, extra
2 large bananas (460g), sliced thinly
500ml vanilla ice-cream
½ cup (40g) toasted almond flakes

1 Stir cream, butter and sugar in small pan, over medium heat, until smooth. Reduce heat; simmer, uncovered, 2 minutes. Cool 10 minutes.
2 Meanwhile, beat extra cream in small bowl with electric mixer until soft peaks form.
3 Divide half of the sauce among four serving dishes; top with banana, cream and ice-cream then remaining sauce and nuts.

preparation time 10 minutes
cooking time 10 minutes
serves 4

LEMON MERINGUE SUNDAE

SUMMER BERRY SUNDAE

STRAWBERRY MILKSHAKE

SPICED ICED COFFEE MILKSHAKE

Milkshakes and malts are both popular soda fountain drinks, the difference being that malts include malted milk powder which gives a distinctive slightly sour flavour. Thick, creamy and delicious, American milk-shakes are usually prepared and mixed by hand, using scoops of ice cream, flavour-ing and milk in a blender.

Milkshakes & malts

SPICED ICED COFFEE MILKSHAKE

½ cup (20g) ground espresso coffee
¾ cup (180ml) boiling water
2 cardamom pods, bruised
¼ teaspoon ground cinnamon
1 tablespoon brown sugar
3 scoops (375ml) low-fat vanilla ice-cream
2½ cups (625ml) no-fat milk

1 Place coffee then the water in coffee plunger; stand 2 minutes before plunging. Pour coffee into small heatproof bowl with cardamom, cinnamon and sugar; stir to dissolve sugar then cool 10 minutes.
2 Strain mixture through fine sieve into blender or processor; process with ice-cream and milk until smooth; serve immediately.

preparation time 5 minutes
(plus cooling time)
makes 1 litre (4 cups)
per 250ml 3g fat; 640kJ (153 cal)

STRAWBERRY MILKSHAKE

250g strawberries, chopped coarsely
2 cups (500ml) milk
2 scoops strawberry ice-cream
½ cup (125ml) strawberry-flavoured topping

1 Blend or process ingredients until smooth.

preparation time 5 minutes
makes 1 litre (4 cups)
per 250ml 8.5g fat; 1007kJ (241 cal)

CHOCOLATE MALT

⅓ cup (40g) malted milk powder
⅓ cup (80ml) chocolate-flavoured topping
1 cup (250ml) chocolate ice-cream
2½ cups (625ml) milk

1 Blend or process ingredients until smooth.

preparation time 5 minutes
makes 1 litre (4 cups)
per 250ml 10.4g fat; 1087kJ (260 cal)

ICED MOCHA

1 tablespoon instant coffee powder
1 tablespoon boiling water
2 tablespoons chocolate-flavoured topping
1½ cups (375ml) cold milk
4 scoops (500ml) vanilla ice-cream
½ cup (125ml) cream, whipped
1 teaspoon drinking chocolate

1 Combine coffee and the water in large heatproof jug, stir until dissolved.
2 Stir in chocolate-flavoured topping and milk. Pour into two large glasses and top each with 2 scoops vanilla ice-cream and cream, then sprinkle with sifted drinking chocolate; serve immediately.

preparation time 5 minutes
serves 2
per serving 43.9g fat; 2696kJ (645 cal)

Great American classics

BAGELS

Bagels originated in Jewish communities of eastern Europe and were introduced to the US by immigrants in the 1880s. They are now one of the most popular breads in the USA. Popular flavour additions to the dough are cinnamon, onion, currants, blueberries and rye flour. The classic filling for plain bagels is cream cheese and smoked salmon, topped with capers.

BAGELS

3 teaspoons dried yeast
1 tablespoon caster sugar
½ cup (125ml) warm water
1 cup (250ml) warm milk
3 cups (450g) plain flour
3 teaspoons salt
1 tablespoon caster sugar, extra
1 egg yolk
1 teaspoon water, extra
1 tablespoon poppy seeds
2 teaspoons sea salt

1 Whisk yeast, sugar, water and milk in large bowl until yeast dissolves, cover; stand in warm place about 10 minutes or until frothy.
2 Stir sifted flour, salt and extra sugar into yeast mixture in two batches; mix to a firm dough. Turn onto floured surface; knead about 10 minutes until dough is smooth and elastic. Place into large greased bowl, cover; stand in warm place about 1 hour until doubled in size.
3 Grease two oven trays. Turn dough onto floured surface; knead until smooth. Divide dough into 12 portions; knead each portion into a ball. Press finger in centre of each ball to make a hole; rotate ball with finger until the hole is a third of the size of the bagel. Place bagels about 3cm apart on trays, cover; stand in warm place about 15 minutes until risen.
4 Preheat oven to moderately hot (200°C/180°C fan-assisted).
5 Drop bagels individually into large pan of boiling water; they must not touch. Turn bagels after 1 minute; boil for a further 1 minute, remove with slotted spoon. Return bagels to trays; brush tops with combined egg yolk and extra water, sprinkle with combined seeds and sea salt. Bake, uncovered, about 20 minutes. Turn onto wire rack to cool.

preparation time 50 minutes
(plus standing time)
cooking time 45 minutes
makes 12
per bagel 2.2g fat; 715kj (171 cal)

CRUSTY SOURDOUGH LOAF

1 teaspoon dried yeast
¾ cup (110g) white plain flour
¼ teaspoon ground cumin
1 cup (250ml) warm water
1⅔ cups (250g) white plain flour, extra
1⅔ cups (260g) wholemeal plain flour
2 teaspoons salt
1 tablespoon vegetable oil
½ cup (125ml) water, extra, approximately

1 Combine yeast, white flour, cumin and water in small bowl; mix well. Cover; stand in warm place 3 days.
2 Sift remaining flours and salt into large bowl; stir in oil, yeast mixture and enough water to form soft dough. Knead on floured surface about 10 minutes until smooth. Place in large oiled bowl; cover stand in warm place about 1½ hours or until doubled in size.
3 Knead dough on floured surface until smooth. Shape into 24cm loaf; place on greased oven tray. Cover; stand in warm place about 30 minutes or until doubled in size.
4 Preheat oven to hot (220°C/200°C fan-assisted). Dust loaf with flour. Using sharp knife, make diagonal slashes on loaf, stand 5 minutes. Bake, uncovered, about 35 minutes until cooked. Cool on wire rack.

preparation time 30 minutes
(plus standing time)
cooking time 35 minutes
makes 14 slices
per slice 8.0g fat; 1099kj (263 cal)

Chowder

MANHATTAN CLAM CHOWDER

1.5kg clams
1 cup (250ml) dry white wine
40g butter
1 medium onion (150g), chopped finely
2 bacon rashers (140g), chopped finely
2 trimmed sticks celery (150g), chopped finely
¼ cup (35g) plain flour
3 cups (750ml) fish stock
400g can tomatoes
3 cups (750ml) water
1 tablespoon fresh thyme leaves
2 bay leaves
4 large potatoes (1.2kg), cut into 1cm cubes
¼ cup chopped fresh flat-leaf parsley

1 Rinse clams under cold running water. Combine with wine in medium saucepan having a tight-fitting lid; bring to a boil. Steam, covered tightly, about 5 minutes or until clams have opened; discard any that do not open. Strain clams over large bowl; reserve ¼ cup (60ml) of the cooking liquid.
2 Melt butter in large saucepan; cook onion, stirring, until soft. Add bacon and celery; cook, stirring, 5 minutes. Add flour; cook, stirring, until mixture thickens and bubbles. Gradually stir in stock. Add undrained crushed tomatoes and the water; cook, stirring, until mixture boils and thickens. Stir in thyme, bay leaves and potato; cook, covered, stirring occasionally, about 15 minutes or until potato is tender.
3 Just before serving, stir clams, reserved cooking liquid and parsley into chowder.

preparation time 25 minutes
cooking time 35 minutes
serves 6
per serving 8g fat; 1190kJ (285 cal)

FISH CHOWDER

60g butter
1 large onion (200g), chopped coarsely
2 cloves garlic, crushed
3 rindless bacon rashers (195g), chopped coarsely
¼ cup (35g) plain flour
2 medium potatoes (600g), chopped coarsely
1 litre (4 cups) milk
3 cups (750ml) vegetable stock
600g firm white fish fillets, chopped coarsely
¼ cup finely chopped fresh chives

1 Melt butter in boiler; cook onion, garlic and bacon, stirring, until onion softens.
2 Add flour; cook, stirring, 1 minute. Add potato, milk and stock; bring to a boil. Reduce heat, simmer, covered, about 10 minutes or until potato is just tender.
3 Add fish; simmer, uncovered, about 4 minutes or until fish is cooked through (do not overcook). Serve bowls of soup sprinkled with chives.

preparation time 15 minutes
cooking time 30 minutes
serves 6
per serving 30.6g fat; 2817kJ (674 cal)
tips Dry red wine can be substituted for the white wine but be certain that whatever wine you use you would also consider drinking.

A thick and nourishing seafood soup native to the East Coast of the United States, there are basically two kinds of chowder. The one on which our fish version is based, New England chowder, always contains bacon, potatoes and milk or cream thickened with flour, while the second, Manhattan chowder, is thinner and flavoured with tomatoes.

MANHATTAN CLAM CHOWDER

FISH CHOWDER

Salads & dressings

WALDORF SALAD

4 medium (600g) red delicious apples
¼ cup (60ml) lemon juice
5 trimmed (375g) celery sticks
1 cup (120g) coarsely chopped walnuts
1 quantity mayonnaise (see page 146)

1 Core and coarsely chop unpeeled apples. Combine apple in small bowl with juice.
2 Coarsely chop celery.
3 Combine apple, celery and walnuts in large serving bowl with mayonnaise. Serve salad in lettuce leaves, if desired.

preparation time 15 minutes
serves 4
per serving 63g fat; 2776kJ (663 cal)

POTATO SALAD

2kg potatoes, peeled
2 tablespoons cider vinegar
1 quantity mayonnaise (see page 146)
8 spring onions, sliced thinly
¼ cup finely chopped fresh flat-leaf parsley

1 Cut potatoes into 1.5cm pieces. Place potato in large saucepan, barely cover with cold water; cover saucepan, bring to the boil. Reduce heat; simmer, uncovered, stirring occasionally, until just tender. Drain, spread potato on a tray; sprinkle with vinegar. Cool 10 minutes. Cover; refrigerate until cold.
2 Place potato in large bowl with mayonnaise, onions and parsley; mix gently to combine.

preparation time 20 minutes
(plus refrigeration time)
cooking time 20 minutes
serves 8
per serving 30.4g fat; 1739kJ (416 cal)

CHEF'S SALAD

350g cooked chicken breast, sliced thinly
1 large cos lettuce, torn
3 medium plum tomatoes (225g), cut into thick wedges
200g thinly sliced ham
100g thinly sliced jarlsberg cheese
3 hard-boiled eggs, quartered

white wine vinaigrette
½ cup (125ml) olive oil
¼ cup (60ml) white wine vinegar
2 teaspoons wholegrain mustard
1 teaspoon white sugar

1 Make white wine vinaigrette.
2 Divide lettuce among serving bowls; layer with chicken, tomato, ham, cheese and egg, then drizzle with vinaigrette.

white wine vinaigrette Place ingredients in screw-top jar; shake well.

preparation time 20 minutes
cooking time 25 minutes
serves 4
per serving 44.3g fat; 2537kj (607 cal)

CHEF'S SALAD

A 'signature' dish in the United States, Waldorf salad was created at the beginning of the 20th century by chefs at New York's world-famous Waldorf-Astoria hotel, and proved so popular that it rapidly became a staple in kitchens throughout America.

POTATO SALAD

Dressings

MAYONNAISE

Combine ½ cup (125ml) olive oil and ½ cup (125ml) light olive oil in a jug. Blend or process 2 egg yolks and 1 teaspoon dijon mustard until smooth. With motor operating, gradually add combined oils in thin, steady stream; process until mixture thickens. Stir in 1 tablespoon lemon juice.

preparation time 10 minutes
makes 1 cup
per tablespoon 19.9g fat; 744kj (178 cal)

RANCH DRESSING

Combine ⅓ cup (95g) yogurt, ⅓ cup (100g) mayonnaise, 2 tablespoons buttermilk, 1 crushed clove garlic, 1 small finely grated onion (80g) and 1 tablespoon finely chopped fresh chives in small bowl.

preparation time 10 minutes
makes 1 cup
per tablespoon 3.0g fat; 167kj (40 cal)

THOUSAND ISLAND

Combine 1 cup mayonnaise, ¼ cup (60ml) tomato sauce, ½ small finely grated white onion, 8 finely chopped pimiento-stuffed green olives and 1 finely chopped small red pepper (150g) in small bowl.

preparation time 5 minutes
makes 1½ cups
per tablespoon 13.4g fat; 527kj (126 cal)

MAYONNAISE

RANCH DRESSING

CHICKEN CAESAR SALAD

1 long french bread stick
⅓ cup (80ml) olive oil
2 cloves garlic, crushed
600g chicken breast fillets
4 bacon rashers (280g), rind removed
1 large cos lettuce, trimmed, torn
6 spring onions, sliced thinly
¼ cup coarsely chopped flat-leaf parsley
100g parmesan cheese, shaved

caesar dressing
1 egg
1 clove garlic, quartered
2 tablespoons lemon juice
1 teaspoon dijon mustard
6 anchovy fillets, drained
⅔ cup (160ml) olive oil
1 tablespoon hot water, approximately

1 Preheat oven to moderate (180°C/160°C fan-assisted).
2 Make caesar dressing.
3 Halve bread lengthways; slice halves on the diagonal into 1cm-thick slices. Combine oil and garlic in large bowl, add bread; toss bread to coat in mixture. Place bread, in single layer, on oven trays; toast in moderate oven about 10 minutes or until croûtes are browned lightly.
4 Meanwhile, cook chicken, in batches, on heated, oiled grill plate (or grill or barbecue) until browned lightly and cooked through. Cook bacon on same grill plate until browned and crisp; drain on absorbent paper. Slice chicken thinly; slice bacon thinly.
5 Combine half the chicken, half the bacon, half the croûtes and half the dressing in large bowl with lettuce and half the onion, half the parsley and half the cheese; toss gently.

6 Divide salad among serving bowls; top with remaining chicken, bacon, croûtes, onion, parsley and cheese, drizzle with remaining dressing.

caesar dressing Blend or process egg, garlic, juice, mustard and anchovies until smooth. With motor operating, add oil in a thin, steady stream until dressing thickens. If thinner dressing is preferred, stir in as much of the water as desired.

preparation time 20 minutes
cooking time 35 minutes
serves 4
per serving 76.5g fat; 4661kJ (1115 cal)

CHICKEN CAESAR SALAD

Seafood platter

COLD SEAFOOD PLATTER WITH DIPPING SAUCES

1 cooked large lobster (1.2kg)
2 cooked crabs (650g)
4 cooked crayfish (800g)
16 cooked large king prawns (1.1kg)
12 oysters, on the half shell
3 lemons, cut into wedges

chilli mayonnaise
½ cup (150g) mayonnaise
1 tablespoon water
2 tablespoons tomato sauce
1 teaspoon worcestershire sauce
½ teaspoon chilli powder

mustard & dill
½ cup (150g) mayonnaise
1 tablespoon water
1 tablespoon drained baby capers, rinsed
1 teaspoon wholegrain mustard
1 tablespoon coarsely chopped fresh dill

chilli & lime
¼ cup (60ml) sweet chilli sauce
2 tablespoons lime juice
1 tablespoon water
2 teaspoons finely chopped fresh mint

1 Place lobster upside-down. Cut through chest and tail; turn lobster around and cut through head. Pull halves apart; using small spoon, remove brain matter and liver. Rinse lobster carefully under cold water. Pat dry with absorbent paper.

2 Place one crab upside-down; lift tail flap then, with a peeling motion, lift off back shell. Remove and discard whitish gills, liver and brain matter; rinse crab well. Cut crab body in half; repeat with remaining crab. Rinse well under cold water.
3 Place crayfish upside-down on chopping board; cut in half lengthways. Remove any green matter, liver and back vein from tails.
4 Shell and devein prawns, leaving heads and tails intact.
5 Make any or all of the dipping sauces.
6 Arrange seafood on large serving platter with lemon. Serve with dipping sauces.

dipping sauces Combine ingredients for each in small bowls.

preparation time 1 hour
serves 4
per serving (including sauces) 29.9g fat; 3612kj (864 cal)

Wings 'n' ribs

CLASSIC BUFFALO WINGS

½ cup (150g) mayonnaise
½ cup (120g) soured cream
¼ cup (60ml) buttermilk
2 teaspoons lemon juice
¼ teaspoon hot paprika
1 small onion (80g), chopped coarsely
100g blue cheese
16 small chicken wings (1.3kg)
vegetable oil, for deep-frying
⅓ cup (80ml) hot chilli sauce
80g butter, melted
4 trimmed celery stalks (400g),
cut into sticks

1 Blend mayonnaise, cream, milk, juice, paprika, onion and half of the crumbled cheese until smooth; stir in remaining crumbled cheese. Cover; refrigerate 2 hours.
2 Cut wings into three pieces at joints; discard tips. Heat oil in large saucepan; deep-fry chicken until cooked through, drain. Combine chicken in large bowl with sauce and butter. Serve chicken with mayonnaise mixture and celery.

preparation time 15 minutes
(plus refrigeration time)
cooking time 15 minutes
serves 4
per serving 66.6g fat; 3503kj (838 cal)

AMERICAN-STYLE RIBS

AMERICAN-STYLE RIBS

1.5kg american-style pork spare ribs
1 cup (250ml) tomato juice
2 teaspoons grated lime rind
¼ cup (60ml) lime juice
2 tablespoons brown sugar
1 clove garlic, crushed
1 red thai chilli, deseeded, chopped finely

1 Cut rib racks into individual ribs.
2 Combine remaining ingredients in large bowl; add ribs. Cover; refrigerate 3 hours or overnight. Drain ribs; discard marinade.
3 Cook ribs on heated oiled barbecue, uncovered, until browned and cooked through.

preparation time 15 minutes
(plus marinating time)
cooking time 10 minutes
serves 8
per serving 16.8g fat; 1086kJ (259 cal)

FINGER-LICKIN' WINGS

1kg chicken wings
2 tablespoons tomato sauce
2 tablespoons worcestershire sauce
2 tablespoons brown sugar
1 tablespoon american mustard

sticky dipping sauce
1 tablespoon american mustard
2 tablespoons tomato sauce
1 tablespoon worcestershire sauce
2 tablespoons brown sugar

1 Preheat oven to hot (220°C/200°C fan-assisted). Make dipping sauce.
2 Cut wings into three pieces at joints; discard tips. Combine sauces, sugar and mustard in large bowl. Add chicken; toss chicken to coat in marinade. Cover; refrigerate 3 hours or overnight.
3 Place chicken on oiled wire rack in large baking dish; brush with remaining marinade.
4 Roast, uncovered, about 30 minutes until chicken is well browned and cooked through. Serve chicken wings with dipping sauce.

sticky dipping sauce Combine sauce ingredients in small bowl; cook, covered, in microwave oven on HIGH (100%) for 1 minute.

preparation time 10 minutes
(plus refrigeration time)
cooking time 30 minutes
serves 4
per serving 7.4g fat; 1229kJ (294 cal)

Burgers & hot dogs

CHEESEBURGERS

500g minced beef
1 medium onion (150g), grated coarsely
1 teaspoon dried mixed herbs
2 tablespoons barbecue sauce
½ cup (50g) packaged breadcrumbs
1 egg, beaten lightly
½ cup (60ml) olive oil
4 hamburger buns, cut in half
4 lettuce leaves
2 medium tomatoes (150g), sliced thinly
½ x 450g can sliced beetroot, drained
4 slices cheddar cheese
½ cup (60ml) tomato sauce

1 Combine beef, onion, herbs, barbecue sauce, breadcrumbs and egg in large bowl. Shape mixture into four burgers.
2 Heat oil in large frying pan, add burgers; cook over medium heat about 15 minutes or until browned both sides and cooked through. Remove burgers from pan; drain on absorbent paper.
3 Preheat grill.
4 Toast buns, cut-side up, under grill. Layer bottom half of bun with lettuce, tomato, beetroot, burgers, cheese and tomato sauce. Top with remaining half of bun.

preparation time 15 minutes
cooking time 15 minutes
serves 4
per burger 32.4g fat; 2997kJ (717 cal)
tip Use the best-quality, low-fat minced beef you can find to make these burgers.

HOT DOGS WITH CARAMELISED ONIONS

25g butter
2 large onions (400g), sliced thinly
1 clove garlic, crushed
1 tablespoon brown sugar
2 teaspoons balsamic vinegar
1 tablespoon beef stock
4 thin continental sausages
4 hot dog buns
⅓ cup (80ml) tomato sauce

1 Melt butter in medium frying pan; cook onion and garlic, stirring, until onion is soft and browned. Add sugar, vinegar and stock; cook, stirring, until thick and syrupy.
2 Meanwhile, cook sausages on heated oiled grill plate or barbecue until browned and cooked through.
3 Split each bun in half; fill with a sausage, caramelised onion and tomato sauce.

preparation time 10 minutes
cooking time 20 minutes
serves 4
per serving 14g fat; 1524kJ (364 cal)

CHEESEBURGERS

HOT DOGS

FRIES

Steaks

CHAR-GRILLED T-BONES WITH POTATO PANCAKES

3 fresh long red chillies, chopped finely
2cm piece fresh ginger (10g), grated
2 cloves garlic, crushed
2 tablespoons olive oil
4 x 300g beef T-bone steaks
4 trimmed corn cobs (1kg)
4 medium potatoes (800g), grated coarsely
50g butter

1 Combine chilli, ginger, garlic and oil in large bowl; add steaks, turn to coat in mixture. Cook steaks on heated oiled grill plate. Cover; stand 5 minutes.
2 Meanwhile, cook corn, turning occasionally, on flat plate until tender.
3 To make potato pancakes, squeeze excess moisture from potato; divide into four portions. Heat half the butter on flat plate; cook potato portions, flattening with spatula, until browned both sides.
4 Spread corn with remaining butter; serve with steaks and potato pancakes.

preparation time 20 minutes
cooking time 30 minutes
serves 4
per serving 33.1g fat; 3118kJ (746 cal)

T-BONES WITH BLUE-CHEESE BUTTER AND PEAR SALAD

4 beef T-bone steaks (1.6kg)
2 tablespoons olive oil
100g mixed salad leaves
1 pear (300g), sliced thinly
½ cup (60g) toasted pecans

blue-cheese butter
50g soft blue cheese
50g butter, softened
2 spring onions, chopped finely

mustard dressing
1 tablespoon american mustard
1 teaspoon honey
¼ cup (60ml) olive oil
1 tablespoon red wine vinegar

1 Brush beef with oil; cook on heated oiled grill plate (or grill or barbecue) until browned both sides and cooked as desired.
2 Meanwhile, combine ingredients for blue-cheese butter in small bowl.
3 Place ingredients for mustard dressing in screw-top jar; shake well.
4 Place salad leaves, pear and mustard dressing in medium bowl; toss gently to combine. Sprinkle with nuts.
5 Spread blue-cheese butter on hot beef; serve with pear salad.

preparation time 15 minutes
cooking time 10 minutes
serves 4
per serving 64.7g fat; 3574kJ (855 cal)

CHAR-GRILLED T-BONES WITH POTATO PANCAKES

Mustard & tarragon butter

For a delicious butter to go with your steak, combine 80g soft butter, 2 teaspoons american mustard and 2 teaspoons finely chopped fresh tarragon. Place on piece of cling film; shape into 6cm log, wrap tightly. Freeze until firm; remove 15 minutes before serving.

T-BONES WITH BLUE-CHEESE BUTTER

Thanksgiving

TURKEY WITH TRADITIONAL STUFFING & GRAVY

4.5kg turkey
1 cup (250ml) water
80g butter, melted
¼ cup (35g) plain flour
3 cups (750ml) chicken stock
½ cup (125ml) dry white wine

traditional stuffing
40g butter
3 medium onions (450g), chopped finely
2 bacon rashers (140g), rind removed, chopped coarsely
1 cup (70g) stale breadcrumbs
2 tablespoons finely chopped fresh tarragon
½ cup coarsely chopped flat-leaf parsley
½ cup (75g) coarsely chopped roasted pistachios
250g minced pork
250g minced chicken

1 Make traditional stuffing.
2 Preheat oven to moderate.
3 Discard neck from turkey. Rinse turkey under cold water; pat dry inside and out with absorbent paper. Fill neck cavity loosely with stuffing; secure skin over opening with toothpicks. Fill large cavity loosely with stuffing; tie legs together with kitchen string.
4 Place turkey on oiled wire rack in large shallow flameproof baking dish; pour the water into dish. Brush turkey all over with half of the butter; cover dish tightly with two layers of greased foil. Roast in moderate oven 2 hours. Uncover turkey; brush with remaining butter. Roast, uncovered, about 45 minutes or until cooked through and browned all over. Remove turkey from dish, cover turkey; stand for 20 minutes.

gravy Pour juice from dish into large jug; skim 1 tablespoon of the fat from juice, return to same dish. Skim and discard remaining fat from juice. Add flour to dish; cook, stirring, until mixture bubbles and is well browned. Gradually stir in stock, wine and remaining juice; bring to a boil, stirring, until gravy boils and thickens. Strain gravy into same jug; serve turkey with gravy.

traditional stuffing Melt butter in medium pan; cook onion and bacon, stirring, until onion softens. Using hand, combine onion mixture in bowl with remaining ingredients.

preparation time 40 minutes
cooking time 3 hours 10 minutes
(plus standing time)
serves 10
per serving 47.4g fat; 3097kj (741 cal)

To test if turkey is cooked, insert a skewer sideways into the thickest part of the thigh then remove and press flesh to release the juices. If the juice runs clear, the turkey is cooked. Alternatively, insert a meat thermometer into the thickest part of the thigh, without touching bone; it should reach 90°C.

TRADITIONAL GLAZED HAM

8kg cooked leg of ham
½ cup (175g) honey
thinly sliced glacé ginger and whole cloves,
to decorate

cranberry-currant glaze
340g jar redcurrant jelly
290g jar cranberry sauce
2 tablespoons lemon juice
⅓ cup brandy

1 Preheat oven to moderate (180°C/160°C
fan-assisted).
2 Cut through rind about 10cm from shank
end in decorative pattern; run thumb around
edge of rind just under skin to remove rind.
Carefully pull rind away from fat up to
decorative pattern.
3 Gently cut diamond pattern into ham
fat (not the flesh); decorate with ginger
and cloves. Place ham on wire rack in large
baking dish; cover shank with foil. Brush
surface of ham with honey; bake, uncovered,
20 minutes.
4 Meanwhile, make cranberry-currant glaze.
5 Brush ham with glaze. Bake, uncovered,
about 45 minutes or until browned all
over, brushing frequently with glaze during
cooking.

cranberry-currant glaze Stir redcurrant jelly
and cranberry sauce in medium saucepan,
over low heat, without boiling, until jelly
melts. Remove from heat; stir in lemon juice
and brandy. Strain.

preparation time 30 minutes
cooking time 1 hour 5 minutes
serves 20
per serving 13.0g fat; 1367kj (327 cal)

PUMPKIN PIE

1 cup (150g) plain flour
¼ cup (35g) self-raising flour
2 tablespoons cornflour
2 tablespoons icing sugar
125g chilled butter, chopped coarsely
2 tablespoons cold water, approximately

filling
2 eggs
¼ cup (50g) firmly packed brown sugar
2 tablespoons maple syrup
1 cup (450g) cooked mashed pumpkin
⅔ cup (160ml) evaporated milk
1 teaspoon ground cinnamon
½ teaspoon ground nutmeg
pinch ground allspice

1 Sift flours and sugar; rub in butter. Add
enough water to form soft dough. Knead on
floured surface until smooth. Wrap in cling
film; chill 30 minutes.
2 Preheat oven to 200°C/180°C fan-assisted.
3 Grease 23cm pie dish. Roll out pastry
between sheets of baking parchment. Ease
into dish; trim edge. Use pastry scraps to
make a double edge; trim and decorate edge.
4 Line dish with baking parchment, fill with
dried beans. Bake 10 minutes. Remove paper
and beans; bake further 10 minutes. Cool.
5 Reduce oven to 180°C/160°C fan-assisted.
6 Make filling; pour into pastry case.
7 Bake pie about 50 minutes; cool.

filling Beat eggs, sugar and maple syrup in
small bowl with electric mixer until thick.
Stir in pumpkin, milk and spices.

preparation time 30 minutes
(plus refrigeration and cooling time)
cooking time 1 hour 10 minutes
serves 8

TRADITIONAL GLAZED HAM

'For pottage and puddings
and custards and pies,
Our pumpkins and parsnips
are common supplies,
We have pumpkins at
morning and pumpkins
at noon,
If it were not for pumpkins
we should be undoon.'
Pilgrim verse, circa 1630

PUMPKIN PIE

As American as...

APPLE PIE

10 medium granny smith apples (1.5kg),
peeled, cored, sliced thickly
½ cup (125ml) water
¼ cup (55g) caster sugar
1 teaspoon finely grated lemon rind
¼ teaspoon ground cinnamon
1 tablespoon caster sugar, extra

pastry
1 cup (150g) plain flour
½ cup (75g) self-raising flour
¼ cup (35g) cornflour
¼ cup (30g) custard powder
1 tablespoon caster sugar
100g cold butter, chopped
1 egg, separated
¼ cup (60ml) iced water, approximately

1 Make pastry; cover, refrigerate 30 minutes.
2 Place apple and the water in large
saucepan; bring to a boil. Reduce heat,
simmer, covered, 10 minutes or until
apples soften. Drain; stir in sugar, rind and
cinnamon. Cool.
3 Preheat oven to 220°C/200°C fan-assisted.
Grease deep 25cm pie dish.
4 Divide pastry in half. Roll one half between
sheets of baking parchment until large
enough to line dish. Spoon apple mixture
into dish; brush pastry edge with egg white.
5 Roll remaining pastry large enough to
cover filling. Press edges together. Brush
pastry with egg white; sprinkle with extra
sugar.

6 Bake pie, uncovered, 20 minutes.
Reduce oven temperature to 180°C/160°C
fan-assisted; bake, uncovered, a further
25 minutes.

pastry Process dry ingredients and butter
until crumbly. Add egg yolk and enough of
the water to process until combined. Knead
on floured surface until smooth.

preparation time 45 minutes
(plus refrigeration time)
cooking time 1 hour 10 minutes
serves 8
per serving 11.4g fat; 1438kJ (344 cal)
tips This slightly cakey (due to the self-
raising flour), very forgiving pastry is a
good one for both pies and tarts, and as
good for tops as bottoms. If you don't have
a processor, rub the butter through the
flours with your fingertips.

PECAN PIE

All-American desserts

PECAN PIE

1 cup (150g) plain flour
90g butter
2 tablespoons water, approximately

filling
3 eggs, lightly beaten
¾ cup light corn syrup or glucose syrup
1 cup (225g) firmly packed brown sugar
30g butter, melted
1¼ cups (125g) pecans

1 Sift flour into bowl, rub in butter. Add
enough water to form a soft dough. Knead
dough gently on floured surface until
smooth; cover, refrigerate 30 minutes.
2 Roll dough on floured surface until large
enough to line 24cm round loose-based flan
tin. Lift pastry into tin, gently ease into side;
trim edge. Preheat oven to moderately hot
(200°C/180°C fan-assisted).
3 Place tin on oven tray, line pastry with
baking parchment, fill with dried beans or
rice. Bake 10 minutes. Remove paper and
beans; bake further 10 minutes or until
pastry is lightly browned. Cool. Reduce oven
to moderately low.
4 Combine filling ingredients in bowl; mix
well. Pour into pastry case; bake 55 minutes
or until set. Cool.

preparation time 25 minutes
(plus refrigeration time)
cooking time 1 hour 15 minutes
serves 6 to 8

STRAWBERRY SHORTCAKE

250g butter
1 teaspoon grated lemon rind
1 tablespoon lemon juice
½ cup (110g) caster sugar
⅓ cup rice flour or ground rice
1 cup (150g) self-raising flour
1⅓ cups plain flour
250g punnet strawberries, halved
½ cup strawberry jam

1 Lightly grease 26cm recessed flan tin.
2 Have butter at room temperature. Beat
butter, rind, juice and sugar in small bowl
with electric mixer until creamy. Stir in sifted
flours in 2 batches. Press ingredients together
gently, knead lightly until smooth.
3 Press dough evenly into prepared tin. Bake
in moderate oven about 20 minutes or until
lightly browned; cool in tin.
4 Turn shortcake onto serving plate, decorate
with berries. Warm jam in small pan; strain,
brush evenly over berries.

preparation time 15 minutes
cooking time 20 minutes
serves 6 to 8

BLUEBERRY CHEESECAKE

250g digestive biscuits
125g butter, melted
250g cottage cheese
250g cream cheese, softened
2 teaspoons finely grated lemon rind
¾ cup (165g) caster sugar
3 eggs
1 cup (240g) soured cream
¼ cup (60ml) lemon juice
300g fresh blueberries
2 teaspoons icing sugar

1 Process biscuits until fine. Add butter, process until combined. Press mixture over base and side of 22cm springform tin. Place tin on oven tray; refrigerate 30 minutes.
2 Preheat oven to 160°C/140°C fan-assisted.
3 Push cottage cheese through a sieve into medium bowl. Add cream cheese, rind and sugar; beat with electric mixer until smooth. Beat in eggs, one at a time, then sour cream and juice. Pour mixture into tin.
4 Bake cheesecake about 1¼ hours. Cool in oven with door ajar. Refrigerate cheesecake 3 hours or overnight.
5 Before serving, top cheesecake with blueberries; dust with sifted icing sugar.

preparation time 20 minutes
(plus refrigeration time)
cooking time 1 hour 15 minutes
(plus cooling time)
serves 12

NEW YORK CHEESECAKE

250g digestive biscuits
125g butter, melted
750g cream cheese, softened
2 teaspoons finely grated orange rind
1 teaspoon finely grated lemon rind
1 cup (220g) caster sugar
3 eggs
¾ cup (180g) soured cream
¼ cup (60ml) lemon juice

soured cream topping
1 cup (240g) soured cream
2 tablespoons caster sugar
2 teaspoons lemon juice

1 Process biscuits until fine. Add butter, process until combined. Press mixture over base and side of 24cm springform tin. Place tin on oven tray; refrigerate 30 minutes.
2 Preheat oven to 180°C/160°C fan-assisted.
3 Beat cheese, rinds and sugar in medium bowl with electric mixer until smooth; beat in eggs, one at a time, then cream and juice. Pour mixture into tin.
4 Bake cheesecake 1¼ hours. Remove from oven; cool 15 minutes.
5 Combine ingredients for soured cream topping in small bowl; spread over cheesecake.
6 Bake cheesecake further 20 minutes; cool in oven with door ajar. Refrigerate cheesecake 3 hours or overnight.

preparation time 25 minutes
(plus refrigeration time)
cooking time 1 hour 35 minutes
(plus cooling time)
serves 14

Classic cocktails

LONG ISLAND ICED TEA

1 cup ice cubes
30ml vodka
30ml tequila
30ml Bacardi
30ml gin
15ml Cointreau
15ml fresh lemon juice
15ml sugar syrup (see page 103)
30ml cola

1 Place ice in 300ml highball glass; add vodka, tequila, Bacardi, gin and Cointreau, one after the other.
2 Add juice and syrup, top with cola; stir.
3 Garnish with a twist of lemon rind, mint leaves, swizzle stick and a straw.

WHISKY SOUR

45ml whisky
30ml fresh lemon juice
15ml sugar syrup (see page 103)
½ egg white (optional)

1 Pour all ingredients into shaker, shake, then strain into 180ml wine glass glass.
2 Garnish with a red cherry at bottom of glass, and lemon slice on side of glass.

DRY MARTINI

45ml gin
15ml dry vermouth
1 cup ice cubes

1 Combine ingredients in a cocktail shaker. Shake vigorously then strain into 90ml chilled martini glass.
2 Garnish with a caperberry or green olive.

SWEET MARTINI

45ml gin
15ml vermouth rosso
1 cup ice cubes

1 Combine ingredients in a cocktail shaker. Shake vigorously then strain into a 90ml chilled martini glass.
2 Garnish with a maraschino cherry.

MANHATTAN

60ml rye whisky
30ml vermouth rosso
1 cup ice cubes

1 Combine ingredients in a cocktail shaker. Shake vigorously then strain into a 150ml chilled margarita glass.
2 Garnish with a maraschino cherry dropped in the glass.

DRY MARTINI

LONG ISLAND ICED TEA

SWEET MARTINI

Just like Mom used to bake

In days gone by in America, the aromas of freshly baked breads, cookies and muffins would regularly greet children back from school and husbands home from work. Nowadays, the cakes and cookies are more likely to be store-bought, but here you'll find a collection of those old traditional American recipes so you can enjoy a breakfast muffin, some cookies and milk, a slice of fruit loaf on the weekend or a slice of warm chocolate mud cake with a scoop of ice cream as an indulgent dessert.

Cookies

CHEWY CHOC-CHUNK COOKIES

2 eggs
295g firmly packed brown sugar
1 teaspoon vanilla extract
150g plain flour
110g self-raising flour
½ teaspoon bicarbonate of soda
125ml vegetable oil
120g coarsely chopped toasted pecans
120g coarsely chopped raisins
150g dark eating chocolate, chopped coarsely
95g white chocolate chips

1 Preheat oven to moderately hot (200°C/180°C fan-assisted). Grease baking trays.
2 Beat eggs, sugar and extract in small bowl with electric mixer about 1 minute or until mixture lightens in colour.
3 Stir in sifted dry ingredients then remaining ingredients (the mixture will be soft). Cover bowl; refrigerate 1 hour.
4 Roll heaped tablespoons of the mixture into balls; place onto trays about 6cm apart, flatten into 6cm rounds.
5 Bake about 10 minutes or until browned lightly. Stand cookies on baking trays 5 minutes; transfer to wire rack to cool.

preparation time 25 minutes
(plus refrigeration time)
cooking time 10 minutes per tray
(plus cooling time)
makes 20

CHOCOLATE CHIP FUDGE COOKIES

125g butter, chopped
1 teaspoon vanilla extract
275g firmly packed brown sugar
1 egg
150g plain flour
35g self-raising flour
1 teaspoon bicarbonate of soda
35g cocoa powder
75g raisins
110g macadamia nuts, toasted, chopped coarsely
95g dark chocolate chips
75g dark eating chocolate, chopped coarsely

1 Preheat oven to moderate (180°C/160°C fan-assisted). Line three baking trays with baking parchment.
2 Beat butter, extract, sugar and egg in medium bowl with electric mixer until smooth. Stir in sifted flours, bicarbonate of soda and cocoa powder; stir in raisins, nuts and both chocolates.
3 Drop rounded tablespoons of mixture onto trays about 4cm apart; press each with hand to flatten slightly.
4 Bake 10 minutes. Stand cookies on trays 5 minutes; transfer to wire rack to cool.

preparation time 15 minutes
cooking time 10 minutes
(plus cooling time)
makes 24

CHEWY CHOC-CHUNK COOKIES

Originally called toll house cookies, choc chip cookies were invented by the owner of the Toll House Inn, Ruth Graves Wakefield, in 1930s Massachusetts. She added bits of dark chocolate to her cookie dough, expecting them to melt during baking. Instead, the chocolate held its shape but became delicate and creamy – and the classic choc chip cookie was born.

CHOCOLATE CHIP FUDGE COOKIES

BROWN SUGAR & PECAN COOKIES

200g butter, softened
½ teaspoon vanilla extract
1 cup (220g) firmly packed brown sugar
1 egg
½ cup (60g) coarsely chopped pecans
1¾ cups (260g) plain flour
½ teaspoon bicarbonate of soda

1 Preheat oven to 170°C/150°C fan-assisted. Grease oven trays; line with baking parchment.
2 Beat butter, extract, brown sugar and egg in small bowl with electric mixer until light and fluffy. Transfer mixture to medium bowl; add pecans. Stir in sifted flour and soda, in two batches.
3 Roll level tablespoons of dough into balls; place about 3cm apart on oven trays.
4 Bake about 15 minutes; cool on trays.

preparation time 20 minutes
cooking time 15 minutes
makes 30

BROWN SUGAR & PECAN COOKIES

PEANUT BUTTER COOKIES

125g butter, softened
¼ cup (70g) crunchy peanut butter
½ cup (100g) firmly packed brown sugar
1 egg
1½ cups (225g) plain flour
½ teaspoon bicarbonate of soda

peanut brittle candy
¾ cup (100g) roasted unsalted peanuts
½ cup (110g) caster sugar
2 tablespoons water

1 Make peanut brittle candy.
2 Preheat oven to 160°C/140°C fan-assisted. Grease oven trays; line with baking parchment.
3 Beat butter, peanut butter, sugar and egg in small bowl with electric mixer until combined. Stir in sifted dry ingredients and crushed peanut brittle candy.
4 Roll heaped teaspoons of mixture into balls with floured hands. Place about 5cm apart on oven trays; flatten slightly.
5 Bake cookies about 12 minutes. Cool on trays.

peanut brittle candy Place nuts on baking-parchment-lined oven tray. Stir sugar and the water in small frying pan over heat, without boiling, until sugar is dissolved; bring to the boil. Boil, uncovered, without stirring, until golden brown. Pour mixture over nuts; leave until set. Crush coarsely in food processor.

preparation time 25 minutes
cooking time 20 minutes
makes 18

OAT, APRICOT & CRANBERRY COOKIES

1 cup (90g) rolled oats
1 cup (150g) plain flour
1 cup (220g) caster sugar
2 teaspoons ground cinnamon
¼ cup (35g) dried cranberries
⅓ cup (55g) finely chopped dried apricots
½ cup (70g) slivered almonds
125g butter
2 tablespoons golden syrup
½ teaspoon bicarbonate of soda
1 tablespoon boiling water

1 Preheat oven to low (150°C/130°C fan-assisted). Grease oven trays; line with baking parchment.
2 Combine oats, flour, sugar, cinnamon, dried fruit and nuts in large bowl.
3 Melt butter with golden syrup in small pan over low heat; add combined soda and boiling water. Stir mixture into dry ingredients.
4 Roll level tablespoons of mixture into balls, place on trays 5cm apart; flatten with hand. Bake about 20 minutes; cool cookies on trays.

preparation time 15 minutes
cooking time 25 minutes
makes 36

Muffins

WHITE CHOCOLATE & MACADAMIA MUFFINS

2 cups (300g) self-raising flour
⅔ cup (150g) caster sugar
¾ cup (140g) white chocolate chips
½ cup (75g) coarsely chopped roasted macadamias
60g butter, melted
¾ cup (180ml) milk
1 egg

1 Preheat oven to 200°C/180°C fan-assisted. Grease 6-hole large (¾-cup/180ml) muffin pan.
2 Sift flour and sugar into large bowl; stir in remaining ingredients. Do not over-mix. Spoon mixture into pan holes.
3 Bake muffins about 25 minutes. Stand muffins in pan 5 minutes; turn, top-side up, onto wire rack to cool.

preparation time 10 minutes
baking time 25 minutes
makes 6

CHOC-BROWNIE MUFFINS

2 cups (300g) self-raising flour
⅓ cup (35g) cocoa powder
⅓ cup (75g) caster sugar
60g butter, melted
½ cup (95g) dark chocolate chips
½ cup (75g) coarsely chopped pistachios
½ cup (165g) chocolate hazelnut spread
1 egg
¾ cup (180ml) milk
½ cup (120g) soured cream

1 Preheat oven to 200°C/180°C fan-assisted. Grease 12-hole (⅓-cup/80ml) muffin pan.
2 Sift dry ingredients into large bowl; stir in remaining ingredients. Do not over-mix. Spoon mixture into pan holes.
3 Bake muffins about 20 minutes. Stand muffins in pan 5 minutes; turn, top-side up, onto wire rack to cool.

preparation time 15 minutes
cooking time 20 minutes
makes 12

FRUIT & SPICE MUFFINS

3 cups (450g) self-raising flour
2 teaspoons mixed spice
½ cup (110g) caster sugar
125g butter, chopped
1 cup (250ml) milk
2 eggs
1 cup (190g) mixed dried fruit

1 Preheat oven to 200°C/180°C fan-assisted. Grease 12-hole (½-cup/80ml) muffin pan.
2 Sift flour, spice and sugar into large bowl; rub in butter. Stir in milk, eggs and fruit until just combined. Do not over-mix. Spoon mixture into pan holes.
3 Bake muffins about 20 minutes. Stand muffins in pan 5 minutes; turn, top-side up, onto wire rack to cool.

preparation time 15 minutes
cooking time 20 minutes
makes 12

CHOCOLATE BROWNIE MUFFINS

We've all now got used to the idea of American-style muffins, sold in every supermarket, coffee bar and café. They began life as a yeast bread but evolved to be a cross between a bread and a cake, with baking powder now being used instead of yeast. They can be flavoured with everything from fruits to chocolate, served hot or cold and can be sweet or savoury.

WHITE CHOCOLATE & MACADAMIA MUFFISS

BLUEBERRY MUFFINS

2½ cups (375g) self-raising flour
90g butter, chopped
1 cup (220g) caster sugar
1¼ cups (310ml) buttermilk
1 egg, beaten lightly
200g fresh or frozen blueberries

1 Preheat oven to 180°C/160°C fan-assisted.
Grease 12-hole (⅓-cup/80ml) muffin pan.
2 Sift flour into large bowl; rub in butter with
fingers. Stir in sugar, buttermilk and egg.
Do not over-mix; mixture should be lumpy.
Add blueberries; stir through gently. Spoon
mixture into pan holes.

3 Bake about 20 minutes. Stand muffins in
pan 5 minutes; turn, top-side up, onto wire
rack to cool.

preparation time 10 minutes
cooking time 20 minutes
makes 12

BERRY & YOGURT MUFFINS

1½ cups (225g) self-raising flour
⅓ cup (30g) rolled oats
3 eggs
¾ cup (165g) firmly packed brown sugar
¾ cup (200g) natural yogurt
⅓ cup (80ml) vegetable oil
180g fresh or frozen berries

1 Preheat oven to 200°C/180°C fan-assisted. Grease six-hole large (¾-cup/180ml) muffin pan.
2 Sift flour into medium bowl. Stir in oats, eggs, sugar, yogurt and oil, then berries. Do not over-mix. Spoon mixture into pan holes.
3 Bake muffins about 25 minutes. Stand muffins in pan 5 minutes; turn, top-side up, onto wire rack to cool.

preparation time 10 minutes
cooking time 25 minutes
makes 6

BERRY & YOGURT MUFFINS

BANANA & CINNAMON MUFFINS

2 cups (300g) self-raising flour
⅓ cup (50g) plain flour
1 teaspoon ground cinnamon
½ teaspoon bicarbonate of soda
½ cup (110g) firmly packed brown sugar
1 cup mashed banana
2 eggs
¾ cup (180ml) buttermilk
⅓ cup (80ml) vegetable oil
½ teaspoon ground cinnamon, extra

cream cheese frosting
125g cream cheese, softened
¼ cup (40g) icing sugar

1 Preheat oven to 200°C/180°C fan-assisted. Grease 12-hole (⅓-cup/80ml) muffin pan.
2 Sift flours, cinnamon, soda and sugar into large bowl; stir in banana, eggs, buttermilk and oil. Do not over-mix. Spoon mixture into pan holes.
3 Bake muffins about 20 minutes. Stand muffins in pan 5 minutes; turn, top-side up, onto wire rack to cool.
4 Meanwhile, make cream cheese topping.
5 Spread topping over muffins, sprinkle with extra cinnamon.

cream cheese frosting Beat cream cheese with sugar in small bowl with electric mixer until smooth.

preparation time 20 minutes
cooking time 20 minutes
makes 12

Brownies & blondies

PECAN & CHOCOLATE BROWNIES

80g butter, chopped
150g dark eating chocolate, chopped
¾ cup (165g) firmly packed brown sugar
2 eggs, beaten lightly
1 teaspoon vanilla extract
⅔ cup (100g) plain flour
1 tablespoon cocoa powder
50g dark eating chocolate, chopped, extra
¼ cup (30g) chopped pecans

1 Preheat oven to moderately hot (200°C/ 180°C fan-assisted). Grease eight holes of a 12-hole (⅓-cup/80ml) muffin pan; line bases with rounds of baking parchment.
2 Combine butter, chocolate and sugar in medium heavy-based saucepan; stir over low heat until smooth.
3 Transfer mixture to large bowl; stir in egg, extract, sifted flour and cocoa, then extra chocolate. Divide mixture among holes of prepared pan. Sprinkle with nuts; bake in moderately hot oven about 20 minutes. Stand muffins in pan for a few minutes before turning onto wire rack to cool.

preparation time 15 minutes
cooking time 25 minutes
makes 8
tip Brownies can be made three days ahead; store in an airtight container.

CHOCOLATE FUDGE BROWNIES

150g butter, chopped coarsely
300g dark eating chocolate, chopped coarsely
1½ cups (330g) firmly packed brown sugar
3 eggs
1 teaspoon vanilla extract
¾ cup (110g) plain flour
¾ cup (140g) dark chocolate chips
½ cup (120g) soured cream
¾ cup (110g) roasted macadamias, chopped coarsely

1 Preheat oven to 180°C/160°C fan-assisted. Grease 19cm x 29cm slice tin; line with baking parchment, extending paper 2cm over sides.
2 Stir butter and dark chocolate in medium saucepan over low heat until smooth. Cool 10 minutes.
3 Stir sugar, eggs and extract into chocolate mixture, then sifted flour, chocolate chips, soured cream and nuts. Spread mixture into tin.
4 Bake brownies 40 minutes. Cover tin with foil; bake further 20 minutes. Cool in tin before cutting.

preparation time 20 minutes
cooking time 1 hour 5 minutes
makes 20

PECAN & CHOCOLATE BROWNIES

CHOCOLATE FUDGE BROWNIES

The Brownie is definitely an all-American favourite. The name refers to its dark brown colour and the beauty of a brownie is that it can be made using just one bowl. They are wonderful plain or served as a dessert with a scoop of vanilla ice cream. Blondies are obviously just a paler relation of a brownie.

TRIPLE CHOC BROWNIES

125g butter, chopped coarsely
200g dark eating chocolate, chopped coarsely
½ cup (110g) caster sugar
2 eggs
1¼ cups (185g) plain flour
150g white eating chocolate, chopped coarsely
100g milk eating chocolate, chopped coarsely

1 Preheat oven to 180°C/160°C fan-assisted. Grease deep 19cm-square cake tin; line with baking parchment, extending paper 2cm over sides.
2 Stir butter and dark chocolate in medium saucepan over low heat until smooth. Cool 10 minutes.
3 Stir sugar and eggs into chocolate mixture, then sifted flour and white and milk chocolates. Spread mixture into tin.
4 Bake brownies about 35 minutes. Cool in tin before cutting.

preparation time 20 minutes
cooking time 40 minutes
makes 16
tips If you like your brownies really chewy, bake them for less time. Before serving dust the brownies with a little sifted cocoa powder or icing sugar, or both.

WHITE CHOCOLATE, NUT & BERRY BLONDIES

125g butter, chopped coarsely
300g white eating chocolate, chopped coarsely
¾ cup (165g) caster sugar
2 eggs
¾ cup (110g) plain flour
½ cup (75g) self-raising flour
½ cup (75g) coarsely chopped roasted macadamias
150g fresh or frozen raspberries

1 Preheat oven to 180°C/160°C fan-assisted. Grease 23cm-square slab cake tin; line with baking parchment, extending paper 2cm over sides.
2 Stir butter and two-thirds of the chocolate in medium saucepan over low heat until smooth. Cool 10 minutes.
3 Stir sugar and eggs into chocolate mixture, then sifted flours, remaining chocolate, nuts and berries. Spread mixture into tin.
4 Bake blondies about 40 minutes. Cool in tin before cutting.

preparation time 20 minutes
cooking time 45 minutes
makes 25
tips Macadamia nuts have a high fat content and should be kept, covered, in the refrigerator to prevent them becoming rancid. You can use other roasted nuts, such as pecans, almonds or walnuts, if you prefer, to use in place of the macadamias. Leave the nuts and berries out of this recipe if you just want a plain blondie.

TRIPLE CHOCOLATE BROWNIES

WHITE CHOCOLATE, NUT & BERRY BLONDIES

Despite the richness of these seriously chocolatey brownies, nobody we know can stop at one. It's great to think that something so good is so easy to make – all in one bowl.

Cupcakes

ROCKY ROAD CUPCAKES

125g butter, softened
½ teaspoon vanilla extract
⅔ cup (150g) caster sugar
2 eggs
1¼ cups (185g) self-raising flour
⅓ cup (80ml) milk
pink food colouring
1 tablespoon cocoa powder
2 teaspoons milk, extra
50g milk eating chocolate, melted

rocky road topping
½ cup (70g) unsalted roasted peanuts
1 cup (200g) red glacé cherries, halved
1 cup (100g) pink and white marshmallows,
chopped coarsely
½ cup (25g) flaked coconut, toasted
200g milk eating chocolate, melted

1 Preheat oven to 180°C/160°C fan-assisted.
Line 6-hole large (¾-cup/180ml) muffin pan
with paper cases.
2 Beat butter, extract, sugar and eggs with
electric mixer until light and fluffy. Stir in
sifted flour and milk in two batches.
3 Divide mixture evenly among three bowls.
Tint one mixture pink. Blend sifted cocoa
with extra milk in cup; stir into another
mixture. Leave third mixture plain. Drop
alternate spoonfuls of the mixtures into
cases. Pull a skewer backwards and forwards
through mixtures for a marbled effect;
smooth surface.
4 Bake cakes about 30 minutes. Turn cakes,
top-side up, onto wire rack to cool.

The term cupcake is probably a reference to the original recipe for the cake mixture — a cupful of butter, a cupful of flour, sugar... Or it's possible that the name also refers to the cups in which they were baked — most tea cups are fired at much higher temperatures than a domestic oven can ever achieve, so are quite safe as baking dishes.

5 Combine ingredients for rocky road
topping in medium bowl. Place topping
on tops of cakes; drizzle with melted milk
chocolate.

preparation time 25 minutes
cooking time 30 minutes
makes 6

CARROT CUPCAKES WITH MAPLE FROSTING

½ cup (125ml) vegetable oil
3 eggs
1½ cups (225g) self-raising flour
1 cup (220g) firmly packed brown sugar
2 teaspoons mixed spice
2 cups (480g) firmly packed coarsely grated carrot
¾ cup (90g) coarsely chopped roasted pecans
12 roasted pecan halves

maple cream cheese frosting
30g unsalted butter, softened
80g cream cheese, softened
2 tablespoons maple syrup
1¼ cups (200g) icing sugar

1 Preheat oven to 180°C/160°C fan-assisted. Line 12-hole (⅓-cup/80ml) muffin pan with paper cases.
2 Combine oil, eggs, sifted flour, sugar and spice in medium bowl; stir in carrot and chopped pecans. Divide mixture among paper cases.
3 Bake cakes about 30 minutes. Stand cakes 5 minutes before turning, top-side up, onto wire rack to cool.
4 Meanwhile, make maple cream cheese frosting. Spread frosting over cupcakes; top each with a nut half.

maple cream cheese frosting Beat butter, cream cheese and syrup in small bowl with electric mixer until light and fluffy. Gradually beat in sifted icing sugar, beating until frosting is spreadable.

preparation time 30 minutes
cooking time 30 minutes
makes 12

Chocolate cakes

CHOCOLATE MUD CAKE WITH CHILLI CHERRIES

250g butter, chopped
200g dark eating chocolate, chopped coarsely
2 cups (440g) caster sugar
1 cup (250ml) milk
1 teaspoon vanilla extract
⅓ cup (80ml) bourbon
1½ cups (225g) plain flour
¼ cup (35g) self-raising flour
¼ cup (25g) cocoa powder
2 eggs

chilli cherries
2 cups (500ml) water
¾ cup (165g) caster sugar
1 small red thai chilli, halved lengthways
1 star anise
6 black peppercorns
10cm piece orange peel
300g frozen cherries

dark chocolate ganache
⅓ cup (80ml) double cream
200g dark eating chocolate, chopped coarsely

1 Preheat oven to 170°C/150°C fan-assisted. Grease deep 22cm-round cake tin; line base with baking parchment.
2 Combine butter, chocolate, sugar, milk, extract and bourbon in medium saucepan; stir over low heat until smooth. Transfer mixture to large bowl; cool 15 minutes. Whisk in sifted flours and cocoa, then eggs.

3 Pour mixture into prepared tin; bake for about 1½ hours.
4 Meanwhile, make chilli cherries.
5 Stand cake 5 minutes; turn, top-side up, onto wire rack to cool.
6 Meanwhile, make dark chocolate ganache.
7 Spread cold cake with ganache; serve with chilli cherries.

chilli cherries Stir the water, sugar, chilli, star anise, peppercorns and peel in medium saucepan over low heat, without boiling, until sugar dissolves. Bring to the boil; boil 2 minutes. Add cherries; simmer 5 minutes or until cherries are tender. Cool cherries in syrup. Remove cherries from pan with a slotted spoon; bring syrup to the boil. Boil 10 minutes or until syrup thickens slightly; cool. Return cherries to pan.

dark chocolate ganache Bring cream to the boil in small saucepan. Remove from heat; add chocolate, stir until smooth.

preparation time 25 minutes
cooking time 1 hour 35 minutes (plus cooling time)
serves 12

The Aztecs first combined chocolate and chilli about 2600 years ago, and the tradition has continued to this day. Bourbon is a traditional ingredient in this recipe, but you can use any other type of whisky or even brandy rum or sherry. If you don't want to use alcohol, use the same amount of milk instead.

DEVIL'S FOOD CAKE

Devil's food cake, a moist, airy, rich chocolate layer cake, is considered the counterpart to the pale angel food cake (see page 190) and most certainly seems the more wicked of the two, with its calorific extravaganza of chocolate frosting and whipped cream.

WHITE CHOCOLATE CARAMEL MUD CAKE

DEVIL'S FOOD CAKE

185g butter, softened
13/4 cups (385g) caster sugar
3 eggs
1½ cups (225g) self-raising flour
½ cup (75g) plain flour
½ teaspoon bicarbonate of soda
⅔ cup (70g) cocoa powder
3 teaspoons instant coffee granules
½ teaspoon red food colouring
½ cup (125ml) water
½ cup (125ml) milk
300ml whipping cream, whipped

rich chocolate frosting
60g dark eating chocolate, chopped coarsely
60g butter, chopped

1 Preheat oven to 180°C/160°C fan-assisted. Grease two deep 20cm-round cake tins; line bases with baking parchment.
2 Beat butter and sugar in small bowl with electric mixer until light and fluffy. Beat in eggs, one at a time. Transfer mixture to large bowl; fold in sifted flours, soda and cocoa with combined coffee, colouring, water and milk, in two batches. Pour mixture into tins.
3 Bake about 45 minutes. Turn cakes, top-side up, onto wire racks to cool.
4 Meanwhile, make rich chocolate frosting.
5 Join cold cakes with whipped cream; top with frosting.

rich chocolate frosting Stir chocolate and butter in small heatproof bowl over small saucepan of simmering water until smooth. Cool at room temperature until spreadable, stirring occasionally.

preparation time 20 minutes
cooking time 45 minutes
serves 10

WHITE CHOCOLATE CARAMEL MUD CAKE

180g white eating chocolate, chopped coarsely
185g butter, chopped coarsely
1 cup (220g) firmly packed brown sugar
½ cup (80ml) golden syrup
1 cup (250ml) milk
1½ cups (225g) plain flour
½ cup (75g) self-raising flour
2 eggs

white chocolate ganache
½ cup (125ml) double cream
360g white eating chocolate, chopped coarsely

1 Preheat oven to 160°C/140°C fan-assisted. Grease deep 22cm-round cake tin; line base and side with baking parchment.
2 Stir chocolate, butter, sugar, syrup and milk in large saucepan over low heat until smooth. Cool 15 minutes. Whisk sifted flours and eggs into chocolate mixture; pour into tin.
3 Bake cake about 1½ hours. Cool cake in tin.
4 Meanwhile, make white chocolate ganache.
5 Turn cake, top-side up, onto serving plate; spread with ganache.

white chocolate ganache Bring cream to the boil in small saucepan, remove from heat; add chocolate, stir until smooth. Refrigerate about 30 minutes or until spreadable.

preparation time 20 minutes
(plus cooling time)
cooking time 1 hour 40 minutes
serves 12

CHOCOLATE BUTTERMILK CAKE

185g butter, chopped
1 teaspoon vanilla extract
1½ cups (330g) caster sugar
4 eggs, separated
¾ cup (110g) self-raising flour
⅓ cup (35g) cocoa powder
¾ cup (180ml) buttermilk

chocolate frosting
400g dark eating chocolate, chopped coarsely
250g butter, melted
½ cup (80g) icing sugar

1 Preheat oven to 180°C/160°C fan-assisted. Grease deep 20cm-round cake tin; line base with baking parchment.
2 Beat butter, extract and sugar in small bowl with electric mixer until light and fluffy. Beat in egg yolks, one at a time. Transfer mixture to large bowl; stir in sifted flour and cocoa, and buttermilk.
3 Beat egg whites in small bowl with electric mixer until soft peaks form; fold into cake mixture, in two batches. Pour cake mixture into tin.
4 Bake cake about 1 hour. Cool cake in tin.
5 Make chocolate filling; reserve about 1 cup.
6 Split cake into three layers. Place one layer on serving plate, spread thinly with some of the remaining chocolate filling; repeat layering with remaining cake layers and filling. Spread reserved filling all over cake. Refrigerate 3 hours before serving.

chocolate frosting Stir chocolate and butter in medium pan over low heat until smooth. Remove from heat; stir in sifted icing sugar.

Cool filling to room temperature; beat with wooden spoon until thick and spreadable.

preparation time 20 minutes
(plus cooling and chilling time)
cooking time 1 hour
serves 10

CARAMEL CHOC-CHIP MUD CAKES

90g white eating chocolate, chopped coarsely
90g unsalted butter, chopped coarsely
½ cup (110g) firmly packed brown sugar
2 tablespoons golden syrup
½ cup (125ml) milk
¾ cup (110g) plain flour
¼ cup (35g) self-raising flour
1 egg
2 tablespoons milk chocolate chips
2 teaspoons icing sugar

1 Preheat oven to 160°C/140°C fan-assisted. Grease 9-hole (⅓-cup/80ml) muffin pan; line bases of holes with baking parchment.
2 Stir chocolate, butter, brown sugar, syrup and milk in medium saucepan over low heat until smooth. Cool 15 minutes.
3 Whisk sifted flours and egg into chocolate mixture; stir in chocolate chips. Divide mixture among pan holes.
4 Bake cakes about 25 minutes. Stand cakes in pan 5 minutes; turn, top-side up, onto wire rack to cool. Serve dusted with sifted icing sugar.

preparation time 10 minutes
(plus cooling time)
cooking time 25 minutes
makes 9

Sunday-best cakes

ANGEL FOOD CAKE

½ cup (75g) plain flour
½ cup (75g) wheaten cornflour
1¼ cups (275g) caster sugar
¼ teaspoon salt
12 egg whites
1 teaspoon cream of tartar
1 teaspoon vanilla extract

1 Preheat oven to 180°C/160°C fan-assisted.
2 Sift flours, ¼ cup of the sugar and the salt together six times.
3 Beat egg whites in large bowl with electric mixer until foamy; beat in cream of tartar. Gradually add remaining sugar to egg mixture, beating until completely dissolved between additions. Add extract; beat until firm peaks form. Transfer egg mixture to a larger bowl; use a whisk to gently fold in flour mixture.
4 Spread mixture into ungreased 25cm tube cake tin; bake about 30 minutes.
5 Place a piece of baking parchment cut larger than the tin on worktop; turn tin upside down onto bench over baking parchment (the tin should rest on its 'feet', or the tube, above the paper) – do not move tin until cake is cold (the cake will drop from the tin when cold). If necessary, use a metal spatula to ease the cold cake from the tin. Decorate with fresh berries, if you like.

preparation time 20 minutes
(plus standing time)
baking time 30 minutes
serves 10

tip It is essential to use the correct tin for this recipe. A tube tin is a round cake tin with tall, smooth sides and a hollow metal tube in the centre. The tube (which may be higher than the outside of the tin) helps give a more even baking in the centre of the cake. If you can't locate a suitable tin in your high-street cook shop, there are many specialist bakeware suppliers on the Internet.

ANGEL FOOD CAKE

BLUEBERRY CAKE

BLUEBERRY CAKE

3 eggs
1¼ cups (275g) caster sugar
2 tablespoons finely grated orange rind
½ cup (125ml) olive oil
⅓ cup (80ml) milk
1 cup (150g) plain flour
1 cup (150g) self-raising flour
100g frozen blueberries
¼ cup (80g) apricot jam, warmed, strained

1 Preheat oven to moderate (180°C/160°C fan-assisted). Grease deep 19cm-square cake tin.

2 Beat eggs, sugar and rind in small bowl with electric mixer until sugar is dissolved; transfer to large bowl. Fold in combined oil and milk, and sifted flours, in two batches.
3 Pour mixture into tin; bake 20 minutes. Carefully remove cake from oven; sprinkle surface evenly with blueberries. Return cake to oven; bake about 40 minutes. Stand cake 10 minutes; turn, top-side up, onto wire rack to cool.
4 Brush warm cake with jam.

preparation time 25 minutes
cooking time 1 hour
serves 16

CARROT CAKE

Carrots contain more sugar than other vegetables, which may explain their use in cakes and desserts, carrot cake being by far the most popular. The rich cream cheese frosting has become an American classic, even though carrot cakes did not begin to appear in cafés and restaurants in the United States until the early 1960s.

JELLY ROLL

CARROT CAKE WITH LEMON CREAM CHEESE FROSTING

1 cup (250ml) vegetable oil
1⅓ cups (295g) firmly packed brown sugar
3 eggs
3 cups firmly packed, coarsely grated carrot
1 cup (110g) coarsely chopped walnuts
2½ cups (375g) self-raising flour
½ teaspoon bicarbonate of soda
2 teaspoons mixed spice

lemon cream cheese frosting
30g butter, softened
80g cream cheese, softened
1 teaspoon finely grated lemon rind
1½ cups (240g) icing sugar

1 Preheat oven to 180°C/160°C fan-assisted. Grease deep 22cm-round cake tin; line base with baking parchment.
2 Beat oil, sugar and eggs in small bowl with electric mixer until thick and creamy. Transfer mixture to large bowl; stir in carrot, nuts then sifted dry ingredients.
3 Pour mixture into tin; bake about 1¼ hours. Stand cake in tin 5 minutes before turning, top-side up, onto wire rack to cool.
4 Meanwhile, make lemon cream cheese frosting. Spread cake with frosting.

lemon cream cheese frosting Beat butter, cream cheese and rind in small bowl with electric mixer until light and fluffy; gradually incorporate the sifted icing sugar.

preparation time 30 minutes
baking time 1 hour 15 minutes
serves 12
tip You need three large carrots (540g) for this recipe.

JELLY ROLL

3 eggs, separated
½ cup (110g) caster sugar
2 tablespoons hot milk
¾ cup (110g) self-raising flour
¼ cup (55g) caster sugar, extra
½ cup (160g) jam, warmed

1 Preheat oven to 200°C/180°C fan-assisted. Grease 25cm x 30cm swiss roll tin; line base and long sides with baking parchment, extending paper 5cm over sides.
2 Beat egg whites in small bowl with electric mixer until soft peaks form; gradually add sugar, 1 tablespoon at a time, beating until sugar is dissolved between additions. With motor operating, add egg yolks, one at a time, beating about 10 minutes or until mixture is thick and creamy.
3 Pour hot milk down side of bowl; add triple-sifted flour. Working quickly, use plastic spatula to fold milk and flour through egg mixture. Spread mixture into tin; bake about 8 minutes.
4 Meanwhile, place a piece of baking parchment cut the same size as the tin on worktop; sprinkle with extra sugar. Turn hot sponge onto parchment; peel away lining paper. Cool; trim all sides of sponge.
5 Roll sponge from short side; unroll, spread evenly with jam. Re-roll cake, from same short side, by lifting parchment and using it as a guide. Serve jelly roll with whipped cream, if desired.

preparation time 20 minutes
baking time 8 minutes
serves 10

Cheesecakes

BUTTERSCOTCH PECAN CHEESECAKE

150g digestive biscuits
50g butter, melted
500g cream cheese, softened
1 teaspoon vanilla extract
¾ cup (165g) caster sugar
2 eggs
1 tablespoon plain flour
½ cup (60g) finely chopped roasted pecans

butterscotch topping
⅓ cup (75g) firmly packed brown sugar
40g butter
1 tablespoon double cream

1 Process biscuits until fine. Add butter, process until combined. Press mixture over base of 20cm springform tin. Place tin on oven tray; refrigerate 30 minutes.
2 Preheat oven to 160°C/140°C fan-assisted.
3 Beat cheese, extract and sugar in medium bowl with electric mixer until smooth; beat in eggs. Stir in flour and nuts. Pour mixture into tin.
4 Bake cheesecake about 45 minutes. Cool in oven with door ajar.
5 Make butterscotch topping by stirring ingredients in small saucepan over low heat until smooth; spread over cheesecake. Refrigerate cheesecake 3 hours or overnight.

preparation time 25 minutes
(plus refrigeration time)
baking time 45 minutes (plus cooling time)
serves 10

COOKIES 'N' CREAM CHEESECAKE

300g plain chocolate digestive biscuits
150g butter, melted
2 teaspoons gelatine
¼ cup (60ml) water
1½ cups (360g) cream cheese, softened
300ml whipping cream
1 teaspoon vanilla extract
½ cup (110g) caster sugar
180g white eating chocolate, melted
150g Oreo™ cookies, quartered
50g dark eating chocolate, melted

1 Line base of 23cm springform tin with baking parchment. Blend or process plain chocolate biscuits until mixture resembles fine breadcrumbs. Add butter; process until just combined. Using hand, press biscuit mixture evenly over base and 3cm up side of prepared tin, cover; refrigerate 20 minutes.
2 Sprinkle gelatine over the water in small heatproof jug; stand jug in small saucepan of simmering water. Stir until gelatine dissolves; cool 5 minutes.
3 Beat cheese, cream, extract and sugar in medium bowl with electric mixer until smooth. Stir in gelatine mixture and white chocolate; fold in quartered cookies. Pour cheesecake mixture over biscuit mixture in tin, cover; refrigerate about 3 hours or until set. Drizzle with dark chocolate to serve.

preparation time 20 minutes
(plus refrigeration time)
cooking time 5 minutes
serves 12

BUTTERSCOTCH PECAN CHEESECAKE

Cheesecakes can be baked in the oven or the filling can be made with gelatine on a biscuit crumb base and simply allowed to set in the refrigerator. The common factor, of course, is the cream cheese. American cheesecakes are generally baked, and the unbaked variety are often referred to as 'cream cheese pies'.

COOKIES 'N' CREAM CHEESECAKE

Fruity loaves

DATE & MAPLE LOAF

¾ cup (110g) finely chopped pitted dates
⅓ cup (80ml) boiling water
½ teaspoon bicarbonate of soda
¼ cup (90g) maple syrup
90g butter, softened
⅓ cup (75g) firmly packed brown sugar
2 eggs
¾ cup (120g) wholemeal self-raising flour
½ cup (75g) plain flour

maple butter
125g butter, softened
2 tablespoons maple syrup

1 Preheat oven to moderate (180°C/160°C fan-assisted). Grease 14cm x 21cm loaf tin.
2 Combine dates and the water in small heatproof bowl. Stir in soda; stand 5 minutes. Stir in maple syrup.
3 Meanwhile, beat butter and sugar in medium bowl with electric mixer until light and fluffy. Add eggs, one at a time, beating until just combined between additions (mixture will separate at this stage, but will come together later). Add butter mixture to date mixture; stir in sifted flours, in two batches.
4 Spread mixture into tin; bake about 50 minutes. Stand loaf in tin 10 minutes; turn, top-side up, onto wire rack to cool.
5 Meanwhile, whisk ingredients for maple butter in small bowl until combined. Serve loaf warm or cold with maple butter.

preparation time 20 minutes
cooking time 50 minutes
serves 10

SWEET POTATO & PECAN LOAF

200g butter, softened
¾ cup (165g) firmly packed brown sugar
2 eggs
¾ cup (90g) pecans, chopped coarsely
½ cup (40g) desiccated coconut
1 cup mashed sweet potato
1½ cups (225g) self-raising flour
½ cup (125ml) milk

1 Preheat oven to moderately low (170°C/150°C fan-assisted). Grease 14cm x 21cm loaf tin; line base and long sides with baking parchment, extending paper 2cm over sides.
2 Beat butter, sugar and eggs in small bowl with electric mixer until just combined; transfer mixture to large bowl. Fold in nuts, coconut and sweet potato. Stir in sifted flour and milk, in two batches.
3 Spread mixture into tin; bake about 1 hour 40 minutes. Stand loaf 10 minutes; turn, top-side up, onto wire rack to cool.

preparation time 20 minutes
cooking time 1 hour 40 minutes
serves 10

DATE & MAPLE LOAF

SWEET POTATO & PECAN LOAF

Candy & sweet treats

GOURMET ROCKY ROAD

300g toasted marshmallow with coconut, chopped coarsely
400g turkish delight, chopped coarsely
¼ cup (40g) toasted blanched almonds, chopped coarsely
½ cup (75g) toasted shelled pistachios
450g white eating chocolate, melted

1 Grease two 8cm x 26cm bar cake tins; line base and sides with baking parchment, extending paper 5cm above long sides.
2 Combine marshmallow, turkish delight and nuts in large bowl. Working quickly, stir in chocolate.
3 Spread mixture into prepared tins, push mixture down firmly to flatten the top. Refrigerate until set; cut as desired.

preparation time 20 minutes
(plus refrigeration time)
makes 30 pieces

ROCKY ROAD ICE-CREAM SUNDAE

2 x 55g Bounty bars, coarsely chopped
50g baby marshmallows
2 tablespoons crushed toasted peanuts
1 litre vanilla ice-cream
¼ cup (60ml) chocolate sauce

1 Combine chopped Bounty bars in medium bowl with marshmallows and peanuts.

2 Divide ice-cream and topping between four serving bowls; drizzle with chocolate sauce.

preparation time 5 minutes
serves 4

SNICKERS ROCKY ROAD

4 x 60g Snickers™ bars, chopped coarsely
1 cup (35g) Rice Krispies™
150g toasted marshmallows, chopped coarsely
1 cup (150g) roasted unsalted peanuts
400g milk eating chocolate, chopped coarsely
2 teaspoons vegetable oil

1 Grease 19cm x 29cm slice tin. Line base and two long sides with baking parchment, extending paper 2cm above sides.
2 Combine Snickers, rice crispies, marshmallows and nuts in large bowl. Stir chocolate and oil in small saucepan over low heat until smooth; cool 5 minutes.
3 Pour chocolate mixture into Snickers mixture; mix until combined. Spoon mixture into prepared tin, cover; refrigerate about 30 minutes or until set. Remove from tin, trim edges of mixture; cut into 3cm squares. Store, covered, in the refrigerator.

preparation time 15 minutes
(plus refrigeration time)
cooking time 5 minutes
makes 54 squares

SNICKERS ROCKY ROAD

Rocky Road can mean different things to different people, depending on what part of the United States they live in, but it is essentially chunks of soft, gooey marshmallow with crunchy nuts covered in chocolate. It can also be used for a delicious topping for ice-cream.

GOURMET ROCKY ROAD

PEANUT BUTTER SWIRL

CHOC-PEANUT BUTTER CORNFLAKE BITES

CHOC-PEANUT CARAMEL SLICES

PEANUT BUTTER & CHOCOLATE SWIRL

360g white eating chocolate, chopped
½ cup (140g) smooth peanut butter
400g dark chocolate, chopped coarsely

1 Grease 20cm x 30cm slice tin; line base and sides with baking parchment, extending 5cm above long edges of tin.
2 Stir white chocolate in small heatproof bowl over simmering water until smooth; cool 5 minutes. Add peanut butter; stir until smooth.
3 Stir dark chocolate in heatproof bowl over simmering water until smooth; cool slightly.
4 Drop alternate spoonfuls of white and dark chocolate into prepared tin. Gently shake tin to level mixture; pull a skewer backwards and forwards through mixture several times for a marbled effect. Stand at room temperature about 2 hours until set; cut into small pieces.

preparation time 15 minutes
(plus standing time)
cooking time 10 minutes
makes about 72

CHOC-PEANUT CARAMEL SLICES

125g butter, chopped
1 cup (220g) caster sugar
395g can sweetened condensed milk
1 cup (140g) roasted unsalted peanuts
200g dark eating chocolate
20g butter, extra

1 Grease deep 19cm-square cake tin. Fold 40cm piece of foil lengthways into thirds; place foil strip over base and up two sides of pan. Line base with baking parchment.

2 Combine butter, sugar and milk in medium heavy-based saucepan; stir over medium heat, without boiling, until sugar dissolves. Bring to a boil; boil, stirring constantly, about 10 minutes or until caramel mixture becomes a dark-honey colour and starts to come away from the base and side of pan.
3 Working quickly and carefully (the mixture is very hot), pour caramel into tin; smooth with metal spatula. Press nuts into caramel with spatula; cool 20 minutes.
4 Stir chocolate and extra butter in small heatproof bowl over simmering water until smooth; spread chocolate mixture over slice. Refrigerate until set. Use foil strip to lift slice from tin before cutting into squares.

preparation time 20 minutes
(plus cooling and refrigeration time)
cooking time 20 minutes
makes 40

CHOC-PEANUT BUTTER CORNFLAKE BITES

395g can sweetened condensed milk
½ cup (140g) crunchy peanut butter
3 cups (120g) cornflakes
80g dark chocolate, melted

1 Preheat oven to moderately hot.
2 Combine milk, peanut butter and cornflakes in large bowl. Drop level tablespoons of mixture, 5cm apart, onto two baking trays. Bake about 12 minutes; cool on trays.
3 Drizzle with melted chocolate; let stand at room temperature until chocolate sets.

preparation time 15 minutes
(plus standing time)
cooking time 30 minutes
makes 25

Glossary

allspice also known as pimento or Jamaican pepper; available whole or ground.

american-style ribs trimmed, long mid-loin pork ribs; sold in racks of eight or ten.

bagel small, ring-shaped bread roll, boiled in water then baked.

baking powder a raising agent containing starch, but mostly cream of tartar and bicarbonate of soda in the proportions of 1 teaspoon cream of tartar to ½ teaspoon bicarbonate of soda. This is equal to 2 teaspoons baking powder.

barbecue sauce a spicy, tomato-based sauce used to marinate, baste or as an accompaniment.

bay leaves aromatic leaves from the bay tree available fresh or dried; used to add a strong, slightly peppery flavour to soups, stocks and casseroles.

beans

black also known as turtle beans or black kidney beans, they are an earthy-flavoured dried bean different from Chinese black beans (which are fermented soy beans). Most often used in Mexico, South- and Central-America and the Caribbean cuisines, especially in soups and stews.

black-eye also known as black-eyed peas; small beige legumes with black circular eyes. Available dried or tinned.

borlotti can be eaten fresh or dried; a pale pink or beige colour with darker red spots.

haricot small, white, oval beans with a smooth texture and bland in flavour. Require soaking.

mexican-style a canned mixture of either haricot or pinto beans cooked with tomatoes, peppers, onions, garlic and spices.

pinto similar to borlotti, a plump, kidney-shaped, pinky beige bean speckled with brown to red streaks; available canned or dried.

red kidney pink to maroon beans with a floury texture and fairly sweet flavour; sold dried or tinned.

beef

rib eye (scotch fillet) the section of eye muscle which runs through the forequarter.

T-bone steak with the bone in and fillet eye attached.

bicarbonate of soda also called baking soda.

buckwheat flour although not a true cereal, flour is made from its seeds. Available from health food stores.

buttermilk fresh low-fat milk cultured to give a slightly sour, tangy taste; low-fat yogurt or milk can be substituted.

butternut squash sometimes used interchangeably with the word pumpkin, butternut squash is a member of the gourd family. Various types can be substituted for one another.

cajun seasoning packaged mix of herbs and spices can include paprika, basil, onion, fennel, thyme, cayenne and white pepper.

capers the grey-green buds of a warm climate shrub sold either dried and salted or pickled in vinegar brine.

cardamom can be bought in pod, seed or ground form. Has a distinctive, aromatic, sweetly rich flavour.

cayenne pepper thin-fleshed, long, very-hot red chilli; usually purchased dried and ground.

celeriac tuberous root with brown skin, white flesh and a celery-like flavour.

cheese

jarlsberg Norwegian cheese made from cow's milk; firm, with large holes and a mild, nutty taste.

mozzarella a semi-soft cheese with a delicate, fresh taste; has a low melting point and stringy texture when hot.

parmesan a sharp-tasting, dry, hard cheese, made from skimmed or semi-skimmed milk and aged for at least a year.

ricotta a soft, sweet, moist, white, cow's-milk cheese with a low fat content (about 8.5 per cent) and a slightly grainy texture. The name roughly translates as 'cooked again' and refers to ricotta's manufacture from a whey that is itself a by-product of other cheese making.

chillies available in many types and sizes, both fresh and dried. The smaller the chilli, the hotter it is. Wear rubber gloves when handling chillies, as they can burn your skin. Removing seeds and membranes lessens the heat level.

chipotle also known as ahumado chillies, they are dried, smoked jalapeños. They have a deeply intense smoky flavour rather than a blast of heat. They average 6cm in length and are dark brown, almost black.

jalapeño fairly hot green chillies. Available in brine bottled or fresh from specialty greengrocers.

powder the Asian variety is the hottest, made from ground chillies; it can be used as a substitute for fresh chillies in the proportion of ½ teaspoon ground chilli powder to 1 medium chopped fresh chilli. chilli thai small, medium hot, and bright-red to dark-green in colour.

chorizo a sausage of Spanish origin; made of coarsely ground pork and seasoned with garlic and chillies.

ciabatta meaning 'slipper' in Italian, the traditional shape of this popular crisp-crusted white bread.

cinnamon stick dried inner bark of the shoots of the cinnamon tree. Also available ground.

coconut, desiccated unsweetened and concentrated, dried finely shredded.

coffee-flavoured liqueur an alcoholic syrup distilled from wine or brandy and flavoured with coffee. Use Tia Maria, Kahlua or any generic brand.

condensed milk a canned milk product consisting of milk with more than half the water content removed and sugar added to the milk that remains.

coriander

dried a fragrant herb; coriander seeds and ground coriander must

never be used to replace fresh coriander or vice versa. The tastes are
completely different.

fresh also known as cilantro or
chinese parsley; bright-green-leafed
herb with a pungent flavour.

cumin available both ground and
as whole seeds; cumin has a warm,
earthy, rather strong flavour.

fennel bulb vegetable, also known
as anise. Also the name given to
dried seeds with a liquorice flavour.

five-spice powder a mixture of
ground cinnamon, cloves, star anise,
sichuan pepper and fennel seeds.

flat-leaf parsley also known as continental parsley or italian parsley.

fruit chutney generally fruit, vinegar,
and sugar cooked down to a reduc-
tion. Various types are available in
supermarkets.

gelatine we used powdered gelatine;
also available in sheet form known
as leaf gelatine.

glucose syrup also known as liquid
glucose.

herbs we have specified when to use
fresh or dried herbs. Use dried (not
ground) herbs in the proportions of
1:4 for fresh herbs, for example
1 teaspoon dried herbs instead of
4 teaspoons (1 tablespoon) chopped
fresh herbs.

kibbled rye cracked rye grains.

macadamias native to Australia, a
rich and buttery nut; store in refrigerator because of its high oil content.

malted milk powder also known as
Horlicks.

maple syrup distilled from the sap
of maple trees found only in Canada
and parts of North America. Maple-
flavoured syrup is not an adequate
substitute for the real thing.

mixed spice a blend of ground
spices usually consisting of cinnamon, allspice and nutmeg.

mushrooms, chestnut light to dark
brown mushrooms with mild, earthy
flavour.

mustard

american mild and sweet in flavour.

dijon a pale brown, distinctively
flavoured fairly mild French mustard.

wholegrain also known as seeded.
A French-style coarse-grain mustard
made from crushed mustard seeds
and Dijon-style French mustard.

nutmeg dried nut of an evergreen
tree; available in ground form or you
can grate your own with a fine grater.

oil

groundnut pressed from ground
peanuts. The most commonly used
oil in stir-frying because of its high
smoke point.

olive mono-unsaturated oil made
from the pressing of tree-ripened
olives. Extra virgin and virgin are the
best varieties, obtained from the first
pressings of the olive, while extra
light or light refers to the taste, not
fat levels.

okra also known as gumbo or lady's
fingers; a green, ridged, oblong pod
with a furry skin. Native to Africa,
this vegetable is used in Caribbean,
Indian, Mediterranean, Middle-
Eastern and southern-American
cooking; it is used to thicken stews.
Rinse and cut off capped end close
to stalk.

oregano also known as wild marjo-
ram; has a woody stalk with clumps
of tiny, dark green leaves that have
a pungent, peppery flavour and are
used fresh or dried.

pancetta an Italian salt-cured pork
roll, usually cut from the belly; used,
chopped, in cooked dishes to add
flavours. Bacon can be substituted.

paprika ground dried red bell pepper
(capsicum); available sweet, smoked
or hot.

peach nectar the (often sweetened)
juice of peaches. If you can't find
the juice in supermarkets, just buy
fresh peaches and blend them to a
pulp. You can add lemon juice, which
will help keep the colour of the
peaches and, unless the peaches are
very ripe, sweeten with a little sugar
to taste.

pecans native to the United States;
golden-brown, buttery and rich.
Good in savoury and sweet dishes;
especially good in salads.

pistachios pale green, delicately
flavoured nut inside hard off-white
shells. To peel, soak shelled nuts in
boiling water about 5 minutes; drain,
then pat dry.

polenta a flour-like cereal made
of ground corn (maize); similar to
cornmeal but finer and lighter in
colour; also the name of the dish
made from it.

raw sugar natural brown granu-
lated sugar.

rolled oats whole oat grains that
have been steamed and flattened.
Not the quick-cook variety.

sourdough so-named, not because
it's sour in taste, but because it is
made by using a small amount of
'starter dough', which contains a
yeast culture, mixed into flour and
water. Part of the resulting dough is
then saved to use as starter dough
next time.

soured cream a thick commercially-
cultured soured cream. Minimum fat
content 35%.

soy sauce made from fermented
soy beans; several variations are
available.

star anise a dried star-shaped pod,
the seeds of which taste of aniseed.

sweet chilli sauce mild, Thai sauce
made from red chillies, sugar, garlic
and vinegar.

sweet potato fleshy root vegetable;
available with red or white flesh.

swiss chard also known as silver-
beet; has fleshy white stalks and
large, dark green leaves. Prepared in
the same way as spinach.

tabasco sauce brand name of an
extremely fiery sauce made from
vinegar, hot red peppers and salt.

tamari a thick, dark soy sauce made
mainly from soy beans without the
wheat used in standard soy sauce.
Used in dipping sauces and as a
basting sauce.

tortillas unleavened, round bread;
available frozen, fresh or vacuum-
packed.

turmeric a member of the ginger
family, its root is dried and ground;
intensely pungent in taste but not
hot or spicy.

vinegar

balsamic authentic only from the
province of Modena, Italy; made
from a regional wine of white trebbi-
ano grapes specially processed then
aged in antique wooden casks to give
the exquisite pungent flavour.

brown malt made from fermented
malt and beech shavings.

cider made from fermented apples.

red wine based on fermented red
wine.

white made from spirit of cane
sugar.

worcestershire sauce a thin, dark-
brown, spicy sauce used as seasoning for meat and gravies, and as a
condiment.

yeast allow 15g compressed yeast to
each 2 teaspoons (7g) dried yeast if
substituting.

Index

american-style ribs 150
angel food cake 190
apple
    apple pie 160
    apricot & almond apple pie 34
    blueberry & apple pies 37
apricot & almond apple pie 34
avocado
    avocado bagel melt 120
    chicken & avocado tortilla
      wraps 52
    corn & courgette fritters with
      avocado salsa 42
    guacamole 46
    mango & avocado salsa 46

bacon
    bacon & corn soufflé omelette
      111
    BLT, Italian deli-style 118
    cheese, corn & bacon muffins 14
    scrambled eggs & bacon 106
bagels 141
    avocado bagel melt 120
    bagels with scrambled eggs &
      smoked salmon 106
    salami & tomato bagel 120
    salmon & cucumber bagel 120
baked beans with fried eggs 13
banana
    banana & cinnamon muffins 177
    banana & maple syrup pancakes
      112
    banana caramel sundae 132
    banana sauce 115
    banoffee pie 130
    buckwheat pancakes with
      caramelised banana 10
    caramelised banana & pecan
      waffles 116
banoffee pie 130
barbecued corn with chunky salsa
    & rice 68
beans
    baked beans with fried eggs 13
    bean & tomato tostada wedges 48
    bean nachos 51
    beef & bean tacos 60
    black bean & chipotle stew 66
    black-eyed bean, beef & spinach
      soup 76
    black-eyed bean, okra & sweet
      potato gumbo 76
    pork & beans 24
    pork & black-eyed beans 83
    spicy corn & bean stew 66
beef
    beef & bean tacos 60
    beef burritos 60

black-eyed bean, beef & spinach
    soup 76
burgers with mustard mayo 125
char-grilled T-bones with potato
    pancakes 154
cheeseburgers 152
chilli burger 124
chilli con carne with corn
    dumplings 62
chilli-beef ribs 65
chilli-rubbed hickory-smoked
    rib-eye steaks 90
corned beef hash with poached
    eggs 138
corned beef with parsley
    sauce 21
empanadas 48
family beef stew 21
fennel-seasoned steak with fried
    green tomatoes 90
gourmet burger 122
meatloaf 18
New York strips with lemon
    thyme butter 127
spiced beef sandwich 118
steak fajitas 54
T-bones with blue-cheese butter
    & pear salad 154
ultimate steak sandwich 127
berry & yogurt muffins 177
black bean & chipotle stew 66
black bottom pie 101
black-eyed bean, beef & spinach
    soup 76
black-eyed bean, okra & sweet
    potato gumbo 76
blondies, white chocolate, nut &
    berry 180
BLT, Italian deli-style 118
blueberry
    blueberry & apple pies 37
    blueberry cake 191
    blueberry cheesecake 165
    blueberry muffins 176
    french toast with blueberry
      compote 108
    strawberry hotcakes with
      blueberry sauce 114
blue-cheese baked potatoes 128
blue-cheese butter 154
brown sugar & pecan cookies 172
brownies
    chocolate fudge 178
    pecan & chocolate 178
    triple choc 180
buckwheat pancakes
    with caramelised banana 10
    with lemon cream 114
buffalo wings 150

burgers
    burgers with mustard mayo 125
    cheeseburgers 152
    chilli burger 124
    gourmet burger 122
    pork chutney burger 122
burritos, beef 60
buttermilk pancakes
    with glazed strawberries 112
    with maple syrup cream 10
butternut squash with walnut
    dressing 30
butters
    blue-cheese 154
    lemon thyme 127
    lime 95
    maple 196
    mustard & tarragon 155
butterscotch pecan cheesecake 194

cabbage, southern-style 96
caesar salad, chicken 147
cajun bloody mary 102
cajun chicken with pineapple
    salsa 84
cajun potato wedges 97
cajun prawns 921
cakes (see also cheesecakes;
    cupcakes; muffins)
    angel food cake 190
    blueberry cake 191
    caramel choc-chip mud cakes
      188
    carrot cake with lemon cream
      cheese frosting 193
    chocolate buttermilk cake 188
    chocolate mud cake with chilli
      cherries 184
    date & maple loaf 196
    devil's food cake 187
    hummingbird cake 98
    jelly roll 193
    mississippi mud cake 98
    sweet potato & pecan loaf 196
    white chocolate caramel mud
      cake 187
caramel choc-chip mud cakes 188
caramelised banana & pecan
    waffles 116
carrot cake with lemon cream
    cheese frosting 193
carrot cupcakes with maple frosting
    183
carrots with orange maple syrup 30
celeriac mash 33
char-grilled prawns with mango
    chilli salad 92
char-grilled T-bones with potato
    pancakes 154

cheese
  avocado bagel melt 120
  blue-cheese baked potatoes 128
  cheese, corn & bacon muffins 14
  cheeseburgers 152
  cheesy sourdough 44
  chile con queso 46
  ham, cheese & tomato melt 120
  spinach & cheese quesadillas 57
  tuna mayo melt 120
  turkey melt 120
cheesecakes
  blueberry 165
  butterscotch pecan 194
  cookies 'n' cream 194
  New York 165
chef's salad 144
chewy choc-chunk cookies 170
chicken
  cajun chicken with pineapple
    salsa 84
  chicken & avocado tortilla
    wraps 52
  chicken caesar salad 147
  chicken enchiladas 59
  chicken pot roast with mustard
    cream sauce 29
  chicken quesadillas 57
  chicken, chorizo & okra gumbo 75
  classic buffalo wings 150
  deep-south wings 84
  farmhouse chicken soup 16
  finger-lickin' wings 151
  homestead chicken pie 29
  jambalaya 88
  southern fried chicken with
    buttermilk mash & gravy 87
  speedy cajun chicken with
    tomato salsa 88
chickpea corn wraps 51
chile con queso 46
chilli & lime dipping sauce 149
chilli burger 124
chilli con carne with corn
  dumplings 62
chilli corn bread 78
chilli dipping sauce 82
chilli mayonnaise dipping sauce 149
chilli pork cutlets with pumpkin
  chips 82
chilli-beef ribs 65
chilli-rubbed hickory-smoked rib-eye
  steaks 90
chimichangas, pork 54
chocolate
  black bottom pie 101
  caramel choc-chip mud cakes 188
  chewy choc-chunk cookies 170
  choc-brownie muffins 174
  chocolate buttermilk cake 188
  chocolate chip fudge cookies 170
  chocolate frosting 188
  chocolate fudge brownies 178
  chocolate malt 135
  chocolate mud cake with chilli
    cherries 184

  choc-peanut butter cornflake
    bites 201
  choc-peanut caramel slices 201
  dark chocolate ganache 184
  devil's food cake 187
  mississippi mud cake 98
  peanut butter & chocolate
    swirl 201
  pecan & chocolate brownies 178
  rich chocolate frosting 187
  snickers rocky road 198
  triple choc brownies 180
  white chocolate & macadamia
    muffins 174
  white chocolate caramel mud
    cake 187
  white chocolate, nut & berry
    blondies 180
chowder
  fish chowder 142
  manhattan clam chowder 142
cinnamon toast 108
clam chowder, manhattan 142
cocktails
  cajun bloody mary 102
  dry martini 166
  frozen tequila sunrise 71
  long island iced tea 166
  manhattan 166
  margarita 71
  mint julep 102
  pineapple & mint margarita 71
  planter's punch 102
  sweet martini 166
  tequila sunrise 71
  whisky sour 166
coffee milkshake, spiced iced 135
cold seafood platter with dipping
  sauces 149
cookies
  brown sugar & pecan 172
  chewy choc-chunk 170
  chocolate chip fudge 170
  oat, apricot & cranberry 173
  peanut butter 172
cookies 'n' cream cheesecake 194
corn
  bacon & corn soufflé omelette 111
  barbecued corn with chunky
    salsa & rice 68
  cheese, corn & bacon muffins 14
  chickpea corn wraps 51
  chilli con carne with corn
    dumplings 62
  chilli corn bread 78
  corn & courgette fritters with
    avocado salsa 42
  corn & courgette salsa 46
  corn bread 78
  crab, prawn & corn cakes 95
  lemon & garlic corn cobs 30
  pork & corn tortilla wraps 52
  scrambled eggs on corn cakes 13
  spicy corn & bean stew 66
corned beef hash with poached
  eggs 138

corned beef with parsley sauce 21
courgettes
  corn & courgette fritters with
    avocado salsa 42
  corn & courgette salsa 46
crab, prawn & corn cakes 95
cream of pumpkin soup 16
creamy mashed potato 33
crusty sourdough loaf 141
cupcakes
  carrot cupcakes with maple
    frosting 183
  rocky road cupcakes 182

date & maple loaf 196
deep-south wings 84
denver omelette 111
devil's food cake 187
dipping sauces
  chilli 82
  chilli & lime 149
  chilli mayonnaise 149
  mustard & dill 149
  sticky 151
dips
  chile con queso 46
  guacamole 46
dressings
  mayonnaise 146
  ranch dressing 146
  thousand island 146
  walnut dressing 30
  white wine vinaigrette 144
drinks (see also cocktails; milkshakes)
  homemade lemonade 38
  peach iced tea 38
  pink limeade 38
drunken beans 38
dry martini 166

eggs
  bacon & corn soufflé omelette 111
  bagels with scrambled eggs &
    smoked salmon 106
  baked beans with fried eggs 13
  corned beef hash with poached
    eggs 138
  denver omelette 111
  eggs benedict 138
  eggs rancheros 42
  poached eggs on sourdough
    bread 109
  scrambled eggs & bacon 106
  scrambled eggs on corn cakes 13
empanadas 48
enchiladas, chicken 59

fajitas, steak 54
family beef stew 21
farmhouse chicken soup 16
fennel-seasoned steak with fried
  green tomatoes 90
finger-lickin' wings 151
fish
  bagels with scrambled eggs &
    smoked salmon 106

fish chowder 142
salmon & cucumber bagel 120
tuna mayo melt 120
french toast with blueberry
    compote 108
fritters, corn & courgette, with
    avocado salsa 42
frosting
    chocolate 188
    cream cheese 177
    lemon cream cheese 193
    maple cream cheese 183
    rich chocolate 187
frozen tequila sunrise 71
fruit & spice muffins 174

ganache
    dark chocolate 184
    white chocolate 187
glazed turkey with cornbread
    stuffing 26
gourmet burger 122
gourmet rocky road 198
gravy 87, 156
guacamole 46
gumbo
    black-eyed bean, okra & sweet
        potato gumbo 76
    chicken, chorizo & okra gumbo 75

ham, cheese & tomato melt 120
hash browns 128
hollandaise 138
homemade lemonade 38
homestead chicken pie 29
honey mustard glazed ribs 81
hot dogs with caramelised onions
    152
hotcakes, strawberry, with blueberry
    sauce 114
hummingbird cake 98

ice-cream sundaes 132
    banana caramel 132
    lemon meringue 132
    mocha liqueur 132
    rocky road 198
    summer berry 132
iced mocha 135

jambalaya 88
jelly roll 193

key lime pie 101

lamb
    lamb pot roast 22
    maple syrup-glazed lamb
        shanks 23
lemon
    buckwheat pancakes with lemon
        cream 114
    carrot cake with lemon cream
        cheese frosting 193
    homemade lemonade 38
    lemon & garlic corn cobs 30

lemon chiffon pie 130
lemon meringue sundae 132
lemon thyme butter 127
lime
    key lime pie 101
    lobster tails with lime butter &
        pineapple mint salsa 95
    pink limeade 38
    tortilla lime soup 45
lobster tails with lime butter &
    pineapple mint salsa 95
long island iced tea 166

mango & avocado salsa 46
mango chilli salad 92
manhattan 166
manhattan clam chowder 142
maple syrup
    baby carrots with orange maple
        syrup 30
    banana & maple syrup
        pancakes 112
    buttermilk pancakes with maple
        syrup cream 10
    carrot cupcakes with maple
        frosting 183
    date & maple loaf 196
    maple butter 196
    maple cream cheese frosting 183
    maple syrup-glazed lamb
        shanks 23
    maple-syrup-flavoured pork belly
        with pecans 24
    waffles with maple syrup &
        strawberries 117
margarita 71
    pineapple & mint margarita 71
martini
    dry martini 166
    sweet martini 166
mayonnaise 146
meatloaf 18
melts
    avocado bagel 120
    ham, cheese & tomato 120
    tuna mayo 120
    turkey 120
milkshakes
    chocolate malt 135
    iced mocha 135
    spiced iced coffee milkshake 135
    strawberry milkshake 135
mint julep 102
mississippi mud cake 98
mocha
    iced mocha 135
    mocha liqueur sundae 132
muffins
    banana & cinnamon 177
    berry & yogurt 177
    blueberry 176
    cheese, corn & bacon 14
    choc-brownie 174
    fruit & spice 174
    white chocolate & macadamia
        174

nachos, bean 51
New York cheesecake 165
New York strips with lemon thyme
    butter 127

oat, apricot & cranberry cookies 173
omelettes
    bacon & corn soufflé 111
    denver 111

pancakes
    banana & maple syrup 112
    buckwheat with caramelised
        banana 10
    buckwheat with lemon cream 114
    buttermilk with glazed
        strawberries 112
    buttermilk with maple syrup
        cream 10
    potato pancakes 154
pea mash 33
peach iced tea 38
peanut butter
    choc-peanut butter cornflake
        bites 201
    choc-peanut caramel slices 201
    peanut butter & chocolate swirl
        201
    peanut butter cookies 172
pear salad 154
pecan & chocolate brownies 178
pecan pie 163
pies
    apple 160
    apricot & almond apple 34
    banoffee 130
    black bottom 101
    blueberry & apple 37
    homestead chicken 29
    key lime 101
    lemon chiffon 130
    pecan 163
    pumpkin 158
    spiced harvest 37
pineapple & mint margarita 71
pineapple mint salsa 95
pink limeade 38
planter's punch 102
poached eggs on sourdough bread
    109
pork
    american-style ribs 150
    chilli pork cutlets with pumpkin
        chips 82
    honey mustard glazed ribs 81
    maple-syrup-flavoured pork belly
        with pecans 24
    pork & beans 24
    pork & black-eyed beans 83
    pork & corn tortilla wraps 52
    pork chimichangas 54
    pork chutney burger 122
    sticky pork ribs 81
    texan-style spare ribs 64
    tex-mex ribs 64
    traditional glazed ham 158

pot roasts
    chicken pot roast with mustard
        cream sauce 29
    lamb pot roast 22
potato (see also sweet potato)
    blue-cheese baked potatoes 128
    buttermilk mash 87
    cajun potato wedges 97
    celeriac mash 33
    creamy mashed potato 33
    hash browns 128
    pea mash 33
    potato pancakes 154
    potato salad 144
    rosemary & garlic wedges 128
prawns
    cajun prawns 921
    char-grilled prawns with mango
        chilli salad 92
    crab, prawn & corn cakes 95
pumpkin (see also butternut squash)
    chilli pork cutlets with pumpkin
        chips 82
    cream of pumpkin soup 16
    pumpkin pie 158
    pumpkin scones 14

quesadillas
    chicken 57
    spinach & cheese 57

ranch dressing 146
ribs
    american-style 150
    chilli-beef 65
    honey mustard glazed 81
    sticky pork 81
    texan-style spare 64
    tex-mex 64
rich chocolate frosting 187
rocky road
    gourmet rocky road 198
    rocky road cupcakes 182
    rocky road ice-cream sundae 198
    snickers rocky road 198
rosemary & garlic wedges 128

salads
    chef's 144
    chicken caesar 147
    mango chilli 92
    pear 154
    potato 144
    waldorf 144
salami & tomato bagel 120
salmon see fish
salsa
    avocado 42
    chunky 68
    classic 66
    corn & courgette 46
    mango & avocado 46
    pineapple mint 95
    pineapple 84
    salsa cruda 54, 60
    tomato 52, 88

sandwiches
    BLT, Italian deli-style 118
    spiced beef sandwich 118
    ultimate steak sandwich 127
sauces (see also dipping sauce)
    banana 115
    blueberry 114
    caramel 116
    hollandaise 138
    lemon cream 114
    maple syrup cream 10
    mustard cream 29
    parsley 21
scones
    pumpkin 14
    sweet potato 96
scrambled eggs & bacon 106
scrambled eggs on corn cakes 13
seafood (see also fish; prawns)
    cold seafood platter with dipping
        sauces 149
    crab, prawn & corn cakes 95
    lobster tails with lime butter &
        pineapple mint salsa 95
    manhattan clam chowder 142
shortcake, strawberry 163
snickers rocky road 198
soups (see also chowder)
    black-eyed bean, beef & spinach 76
    cream of pumpkin 16
    farmhouse chicken soup 16
    tomato & pepper 45
    tortilla lime 45
sourdough
    cheesy sourdough 44
    crusty sourdough loaf 141
    poached eggs on sourdough
        bread 109
southern fried chicken with
    buttermilk mash & gravy 87
southern-style cabbage 96
speedy cajun chicken with tomato
    salsa 88
spiced beef sandwich 118
spiced harvest pie 37
spiced iced coffee milkshake 135
spicy corn & bean stew 66
spinach
    black-eyed bean, beef & spinach
        soup 76
    spinach & cheese quesadillas 57
steak see beef
stews (see also gumbo)
    black bean & chipotle 66
    family beef 21
    spicy corn & bean 66
sticky pork ribs 81
strawberry
    buttermilk pancakes with glazed
        strawberries 112
    strawberry hotcakes with
        blueberry sauce 114
    strawberry milkshake 135
    strawberry shortcake 163
    waffles with maple syrup &
        strawberries 117

stuffing
    cornbread stuffing 26
    traditional stuffing 156
sugar syrup 103
summer berry sundae 132
sweet martini 166
sweet potato
    black-eyed bean, okra & sweet
        potato gumbo 76
    sweet potato & pecan loaf 196
    sweet potato mash 33
    sweet potato scones 96
    sweet potato slices 128

T-bones with blue-cheese butter and
    pear salad 154
tacos, beef & bean 60
tequila sunrise 71
    frozen tequila sunrise 71
texan-style spare ribs 64
tex-mex ribs 64
thousand island dressing 146
tomato
    bean & tomato tostada wedges 48
    BLT, Italian deli-style 118
    fennel-seasoned steak with fried
        green tomatoes 90
    ham, cheese & tomato melt 120
    salami & tomato bagel 120
    tomato & pepper soup 45
    tomato salsa 52, 88
tortilla lime soup 45
tostada wedges, bean & tomato 48
traditional glazed ham 158
traditional stuffing 156
triple choc brownies 180
tuna mayo melt 120
turkey
    glazed turkey with cornbread
        stuffing 26
    turkey melt 120
    turkey with traditional stuffing &
        gravy 156

ultimate steak sandwich 127

waffles
    caramelised banana & pecan 116
    with caramel sauce 116
    with maple syrup & strawberries
        117
waldorf salad 144
walnut dressing 30
whisky sour 166
white chocolate
    white chocolate & macadamia
        muffins 174
    white chocolate caramel mud
        cake 187
    white chocolate, nut & berry
        blondies 180
white wine vinaigrette 144
wraps
    chicken & avocado tortilla 52
    chickpea corn 51
    pork & corn tortilla 52

Conversion charts

MEASURES

» The cup and spoon measurements used in this book are metric: one measuring cup holds approximately 250ml; one metric tablespoon holds 20ml; one metric teaspoon holds 5ml.

» All cup and spoon measurements are level. The most accurate way of measuring dry ingredients is to weigh them. When measuring liquids, use a clear glass or plastic jug with metric markings.

» We used large eggs with an average weight of 60g.

WARNING This book may contain recipes for dishes made with raw or lightly cooked eggs. These should be avoided by vulnerable people such as pregnant and nursing mothers, invalids, the elderly, babies and young children.

DRY MEASURES

METRIC	IMPERIAL
15g	½oz
30g	1oz
60g	2oz
90g	3oz
125g	4oz (¼lb)
155g	5oz
185g	6oz
220g	7oz
250g	8oz (½lb)
280g	9oz
315g	10oz
345g	11oz
375g	12oz (¾lb)
410g	13oz
440g	14oz
470g	15oz
500g	16oz (1lb)
750g	24oz (1½lb)
1kg	32oz (2lb)

LIQUID MEASURES

METRIC	IMPERIAL
30ml	1 fluid oz
60ml	2 fluid oz
100ml	3 fluid oz
125ml	4 fluid oz
150ml	5 fluid oz (¼ pint/1 gill)
190ml	6 fluid oz
250ml	8 fluid oz
300ml	10 fluid oz (½ pint)
500ml	16 fluid oz
600ml	20 fluid oz (1 pint)
1000ml (1 litre)	1¾ pints

LENGTH MEASURES

METRIC	IMPERIAL
3mm	⅛in
6mm	¼in
1cm	½in
2cm	¾in
2.5cm	1in
5cm	2in
6cm	2½in
8cm	3in
10cm	4in
13cm	5in
15cm	6in
18cm	7in
20cm	8in
23cm	9in
25cm	10in
28cm	11in
30cm	12in (1ft)

OVEN TEMPERATURES

These oven temperatures are only a guide for conventional ovens. For fan-assisted ovens, check the manufacturer's manual.

	°C (CELSIUS)	°F (FAHRENHEIT)	GAS MARK
Very low	120	250	½
Low	150	275–300	1–2
Moderately low	160	325	3
Moderate	180	350–375	4–5
Moderately hot	200	400	6
Hot	220	425–450	7–8
Very hot	240	475	9